THE**ALPHABET**GAMES
The Numinous Protocol

Birgit Von Schondorf

ISBN: 1480043877
ISBN-13: 9781480043879
Library of Congress Control Number: 2012918711
CreateSpace Independent Publishing Platform,
North Charleston, South Carolina

"If you have ever wondered what it is like for an undercover CIA operative to work as part of a covert team in hostile environments where a combination of luck, skill and survival instincts are the ticket to living another day- this gritty book is compelling reading"

–a lengthy veteran of the intelligence community and numerous covert missions

"This unique book tells a compelling and entertaining story about survival in a world most of us do not know exists. It is about men and women who quietly put themselves in harms way to protect us and our freedom. A must read."

- Captain W. Trafton, USN (Ret) USS Forrestal combat pilot, NASA

The Alphabet Games, the first in a series, promises to be a winner out of the box. Based on the real world of individual CIA operatives, it reveals how things get done and missions are accomplished, including a reality check in the real world.

You haven't read anything as remotely close to this real life description of one of the most important activities that keeps the United States in the forefront of the battle against the seriously demented who seek nothing less than our destruction. No matter the religion, race, national origin or sexual preference, all of us are targets of these truly evil folks.

There's reason to look forward to the follow up to *The Alphabet Games, The Numinous Protocol.*

Let's hope we don't have to wait too long.

- Dan Calabria Former CEO Templeton Funds, Executive Vice President Dreyfus Funds, industry arbitrator NASD and New York Stock Exchange, Author of : Mutual Funds Today... Who's watching Your money?

Dedication

This is dedicated to former CIA Director General David Petraeus–war fighter and guardian of democracy–whose heroism and extraordinarily selfless nature throughout his military career places him among the ranks of America's greatest patriots since the founding of our country.

To the true patriots, the nameless, faceless, past, present and future of clandestine services here and abroad and to my beloved family and closest friends and country who I could not "be" without.

With Love.

CONTENTS

AUTHORSNOTE

Please understand that the reason that I wrote this book is to feature people and situations that I consider truly remarkable.

The men and women of "clandestine services" are some of the most selfless beings on the planet. Yet, they are in large part the main reason that we have all the things that we as Americans have come to take for granted. Safety, clean and safe water, air, food, safe commerce and travel. Without the openness and access to these staples and the ability to move about the country and the world safely and freely, most Americans would have serious issues.

We have been given the ability to share prosperity around the globe. No other country in history has ever cared for the world on the grand scale that we have. We have always been far from having the largest populous or the oldest established country. Yet, we have paid in an unprecedented fashion into the human race; sweat, brain power, fiscally and with our young blood. Millions of men and women have selflessly shared their best days and some of their worst with everyone on our small blue planet; with little care for where their GPS told them they were standing when they did it.

The lack of mindfulness of these facts and these unsettled times are what launched me into writing this series.

PROLOGUE

"We are the world," I mused, as I ambled by Manhattan's South Street Seaport. I was headed toward Ground Zero. Never mind that it was pouring rain; the inclement weather suited my somber mood perfectly. After all, this was my fourth visit to what effectively was a modern day battlefield, Ground Zero.

The date was September 11. It was getting late, and I was soaked. The area around the hallowed grounds where nearly 3,000 people had been slaughtered nine years earlier was eerily quiet. Even the night shift of hard hats working on the sprawling, muddied construction site behind a tattered cloth and chain–link barrier seemed unusually subdued. I was standing in what was basically a war zone, a new kind of urban battlefield which America was unaccustomed to, and for which it obviously was totally unprepared. I was grateful to be in one piece.

I asked the person that I was speaking to what he thought of an idea I had been contemplating for some time—a series of books about American operatives lives in the Global War on Terrorism, or GWOT (pronounced *gee-wot*). He thought about it for a moment and then he expressed enthusiastic support.

I was impacted by the steel and concrete skeletal structure which was beginning to rise from the dark pit. I remember thinking, 'I don't feel very "We Are The World," the stirring Quincy Jones song written and performed to celebrate, at least in theory, unity. Instead, I found myself wondering, what's wrong with this world? As a country, America is far from perfect but, who could possibly argue the point that America has brought more good and prosperity to the global community than havoc and ruin in the last two centuries—

which is a lot more than I can say for many other nations. For most of America's existence, our intentions have been pure. Talk to any military kid, and they will tell you all about it firsthand.

Americans, for the most part are idealists who come from every imaginable place on the planet. And most made huge personal sacrifices, and in many cases put their life on the line to get here. Why? Because this is where they knew they would get a real shot at making a life for themselves and their families, free from tyranny and political and religious oppression. Today, it is nothing short of a gift to be born here.

As I stared at the Ground Zero pit, I began to perceive a different kind of hole. It became a 'whole,' as in *the whole picture,* and how lately it seemed Americans just weren't getting it. Creeping complacency has become the rule of the day, from schools to offices to farms across this land. Whatever the reason, hand it to Americans, we know where our priorities are—smart phones, "American Idol," and keeping abreast of the latest celebrity's misdeeds.

Now, on this anniversary that was both a celebration of perseverance and a stark reminder of the horrors that exist in the world, I was at this place because I felt I was where I needed to be. It was there at Ground Zero, where I came to terms with my inspiration—to put pen to paper. It was something I had to do for my own peace of mind, and in memory of all the people who suffered on 9/11 and who continue to suffer in the GWOT.

Shortly before this first in a series went to press, I made a pilgrimage to Arlington National Cemetery. The profound experience was like closing a circle since my visit to Ground Zero. There, I looked out over a sea of men and women who had paid the ultimate price in service to their county. There were headstones as far as the eye could see. How at odds the sight of all those grave stones were with the knowledge that we have reached the point where saying the Pledge of Allegiance in the classroom is forbidden, as is uttering the word "God." Why do I not believe that the people in the ground at Arlington had a problem reciting the Pledge of Allegiance. (Arlington should be a class trip for every single middle school child in the United States.)

Sadly, too many Americans have no interest in events of the past, because they are perceived as no longer relevant. Given our current trajectory, history couldn't be a more valuable teaching tool. One of America's founding fathers, Benjamin Franklin, stated, "Those who would give up essential liberty to purchase a little temporary safety deserve neither liberty nor safety."

How applicable to our society in 2012. Looking ahead, it is a moral imperative that we listen to the wisdom of the people who came before us, because our very survival and future of our precious country depends on it. Shame on those who would attempt to make us less than what we are and what we always have been: a beacon of light and hope for the rest of the world.

Birgit Von Schondorf

This is a non fiction work, a true story, gleaned from a compilation of interviews and dialogue that took place over several years. Persons and situations have been altered in the name of safety and national security. The Alphabet Games "The Numinous Protocol" is the first book in a series.

We have the opposite problem, while most of the populous struggles for excitement and creates drama and havoc in their everyday lives in an attempt to relive what they perceive as boredom; we seek normalcy or what we perceive as normal and the safety and peace of mind that go with it.

CHAPTER ONE

Muffled sounds of a third world country course through the wretchedly polluted, bluish air that hung over Islamabad. Mingled with the stench of garbage and excrement, the combination made this city of 1.2 million souls an open-air sewer for anyone unlucky enough to live or have business here.

On this particular day in mid-December, Penn Adams, a CIA operative working under cover, was among the seething mass of people. In an instant, all hell broke loose, and the hunter became the hunted. It was all so surreal, as if the events were happening in slow motion. A violent ballet of chaos—shoving, running, the cacophony of rattletrap automobile horns, and shouting. Penn knew he was in imminent danger, and he broke into a sprint. His heart was pounding so hard that it felt like it was going to burst through his chest. "This can't be happening," his brain screamed out.

His survival instinct kicked in, and he could feel the rush of adrenalin in his veins. He tried to control his breathing, but fear blocked all such efforts. The ringing in his ears made it hard for him to hear; close range gunfire has a tendency to do that. Penn wondered whether he was injured, but he couldn't feel his feet or his bum right knee as he raced down a shitty little side street. Fifty paces behind him, several rag head assassins yelling in Urdu, the official language, pursued and shot at him. This biological stupidity was an issue, because he had just jumped out of a third-floor window. Conveniently, a pile of sand being used by a construction crew cushioned his fall. "What an immensely fucked up day," he thought. He was certain it would be his last. By the time he had arrived in Islamabad, he already had used up more lives than any man was entitled to have. He was working on … five, or was it six? He had lost count. Segments of his life flashed through his mind as bullets whizzed past his head. The sound reminded him of persistent mosquito hovering near the side of his head. You can hear the little bastard, you just can't see it.

Up ahead, Penn spotted an old man tending an ice cream cart adorned with a skirt that reached down to the unpaved street, boxes stacked to one side. Penn ran towards the cart and dove underneath in one motion, praying the bearded vendor would not rat him out to the gunmen who wanted to kill him. Mercifully, they ran past the rickety cart that obscured Penn from their view. The old man was oblivious to the commotion around him. Penn's breathing finally began to slow as he knelt motionless.

But Penn was pissed. The extraction team he had been expecting was nowhere to be seen. When he thought the coast was clear, and while still crouched under the cart, he placed a call to Langley on his small satellite phone. He swore at his handler, Clay, to get him the fuck out of Dodge. Sweat ran down his face and into his eyes. He wiped it away with the handkerchief he kept in a back pocket. Then he instructed Clay to relay a call to Aria. He felt like he needed to hear her voice. In point of fact, Penn wasn't supposed to be calling anyone in the midst of mission. But he wasn't sure he would ever get to talk to Aria or see her again. He had just dodged a proverbial bullet; in fact, by sheer luck he had avoided a hale of them. As far as he was concerned, he had earned the right to break a rule or two. Clay understood and put the call through without hesitating …

Thursday November 5ᵀʰ

It should be a normal day, a day like any other. You get up, rush like hell wake up in the shower, struggle to find coffee, swear when you discover on the way to the car or the train that your stocking has a run in it and you know that you don't have a backup in your bag. This day should be like a mediocre whiny song on the radio which passes for rock now with your average 15 year old in any suburban center in America; but it wasn't. This was his life, her life, their lives, the country's life and the agency's life and there was nothing normal, standard or typical about it. There is no graph or book or sign or special handshake that ensures when people like them find each other, sleep together and fall in love. (There's even less to go on when people like them, whatever those are) discover they are far more connected than meets the eye. (So says the day when they met.) So now let's backtrack a bit and talk about when they weren't. That could be described easily. Madonna–Whore. She was a Madonna and he was a whore. She had not been with anyone for a long time. She had a boyfriend who was the only person she even thought about sleeping with. She was single now after being basically a child bride in an abusive relationship. She was not hot to enter into the bonds of matrimony in this lifetime again…ever! He on the other hand was married and had stayed so out of guilt because of his two lovely daughters. Married… to their mother who he did not like, much less love or sleep with any longer. He was a male whore. Getting some on the side like everyone else in his profession up to double digits a week from a revolving door of four steady women and fillers whenever and wherever. Sport fucking was his only MO.

He was what she now affectionately called a himbo. A male bimbo. Then came that fateful day. "The Day." That summer day in New York that felt like a blast of winter and was totally out of whack. To this day it still doesn't seem real, but surely it is, whether we like it or not. It's real, at times too real. Real all over the world. From the Kremlin to Karachi to Washington to Beijing and marble halls to sunny beaches. From big rooms with too much technology, to men who only have one name and have a closet full of trench coats.

We swear, alot. The stakes are so much higher on a normal day than regular people could ever imagine anyone actually dealing with. Sorry, but much to anyone's dismay this deal does not run on Dunkin. But then again, who ever said that they were normal. Fat chance. Doesn't everyone's boyfriend, best friend, soul mate, possible future husband bolt out of bed to take a call in the middle of the night from Karachi? The short answer is no, no they don't. This is reality, his reality and hers. Aria Mc Connell remembered what it was like before she met the group. Before they knew her and she knew them. Before the meeting that day in NY. Where she knew everything... and Langley knew that, but everyone was doing a damn good job of being in denial. She used to pretend that she was just "some girl." She had gotten the calls years before from family and friends... "so sorry can't make dinner, I'm gonna be late"... and then "boom" an embassy blows up, and a normal Tuesday ends in total denial...

But back to "The Day." One of the "Governor's Boys", a lawyer, a good for nothing, had the "hots" for her and facilitated this meeting with him. It was destiny, it had to happen, that they would work together. She had already been recruited and taken on the project. She was a journalist. She had given her word. She was traveling the farthest, so therefore she arrived early. Up at the crack of dawn, a flight to LaGuardia and a cab into the city. Security was a pain in her ass. Aria wished at other times they would be so vigilant. They put her through everything short of a full body cavity search. She felt like she was flying El Al. Or going to Canada, again. Treated like an Escobarian drug lord you would have thought she was just another hussy blowing someone's boss, but she wasn't. She was there because of a nun. Not your typical issue in threat assessment, nuns. If anyone would have bothered to ask she would have been happy to tell them that she was there because of a nun. When she finally got up stairs to Penn Adam's office, he later confessed that he came to the lobby to spy.

When she finally got into his office he wanted to jump her and she knew it. At one point, months later, he confessed that when she walked around the desk that he had the worlds hardest time not manhandling her and deep kissing her and pushing her down on on the desk. It would have been exactly where her head was at, but he probably would have gotten slapped. She had him by then anyway. He was cocky and scared at the same time, interesting...

Aria knew who she was dealing with, but little did he know. The only thing she didn't understand was the hug after the business lunch. That was him trying anything possible to get near her; short of clearing the table there in the steak restaurant and doing her in front of the lunch crowd.

They were hot out of the shoot from the very first moment and despite the fact that he was so very tuned in because his life depended on it every minute of every day, he was sunk. But he was safe because he was with his ultimate match. Like a sidearm that they built completely for him at Langley. They fit together better than a glove, they were twin cells from different times and of a different sex. Like mirror image twins, inside and out, on a metaphysical level. It was like two beings existing in one skin. Even standing close was like the best sex you've never had, times ten. It was all theirs, and no one else ever had a clue.

It was mind-blowing no matter how you looked at it. She was good with all of it by then; she would have been his biggest fan if he would have pulled a Clark Gable. She can do Scarlet! Probably more Johansen, than O'Hara but you have to be flexible. He told her a month ago that he would have run off to a hotel with her that very moment that lunch was over, if she would have given him a sign. Ah, then she would have been just like any of the other typical tarts he was banging from all over the world that were hoping their husband shopping would come complete with US citizenship inclusive.

The animal had stolen the hotshot lawyer's potential girlfriend that apparently he had been bragging about for months. He had not gotten the memo... that this would take time, several months and two trips to the Middle East, one to the Med, and one to the Ottoman Empire and lastly one moment in Washington. The kicker was getting his chops busted for a relationship with a little blue pill that jumped out of his pocket and on to the carpet, jumping the gun a bit, no?

He left her alone on that first trip, alone in Washington. He was busy freaking out. Run away... Run away. Used to not caring about anyone, not getting it on you. They didn't even have sex, but they wanted to. Aria was glad that they had not yet slept together. Because surely he would have broken her heart, and of course he did. All she remembered was being on the treadmill afterwards feeling terribly hurt, tears streaming down her face while he drove back to New York City. She knew he was scared but she couldn't believe that he actually left her there, alone. Did he have the emotional and mental capacity to be able to handle her? At least he still had no idea what "handling her" was really about, thank God. He was the one with handlers, but she was the one who needed them. She secretly hoped that she wouldn't need to hold his hand too much. She didn't want to be the strong one, the boy. That always made her feel so unfeminine.

She hated it when she had to always take the lead. People were generally so wishy-washy now and so ill informed. Idiocracy with Luke Wilson comes to mind. She hoped that he would be so wildly intelligent that after he saw things for himself, that he would or could understand. Telling her that it was okay to really be herself. She already knew his story, there were just some details to be filled in, but he might vomit, thinking he was completely out of his mind if he really started to understand hers. Let's hope he could recognize the heart in his chest, she did. For them the jury was still out ...

CHAPTER TWO

Sept 14,

Underground bunkers, engines, skeezy low end VC guys and weapons, big money and men that only have numbers as names. What am I supposed to feel? My life is like the movies, only much more real. When I don't brush my teeth I need a lot of mouthwash. That does not happen in the movies, or in the books that I read. The spies in the movies never have bad breath or worry about it. Things always go well, Sean Connery, Roger Moore and Pierce Brosnan and Daniel Craig are always perfect. Every minute of every day, no basis in reality. The real deal is prep... prep, fingers crossed swear...pray. Closely followed by breathing, amazement and sleep. This is the real world, not Pinewood. Her Majesty sold separately.

His name was Penn and he was perfect. At least he was my version of perfect anyway and that was all that mattered. In a perfect world, I could spell and my ass wouldn't be broken. That's not so Hollywood, belly problems based in field stress. Yeah, that's one thing they don't ever show. The big dilemma of the week is how the hell do I introduce all these people to each other without blowing protocol so they can all help each other? Everyone is so sensitive, understandably. I feel like the colorblind kid at Christmas with the Rubik's cube in my stocking.. Duh.

August 16ᵗʰ

Sitting here and it's late. Watching one of my favorite movies, starring one of my favorite actresses Angela Bassett, "How Stella Got

Her Groove Back." Boy did I need this tonight. We are all alive and intact... after these past two weeks... amazing! I am safe, and I have a headache mostly from stress, but it could also be because I have had one hell of a night and a day and I traveled alot and did something that I don't ever do, I drank. I'm a light weight to the extreme. An eighth of a glass of red to calm me down and take away the pain in my head and neck. It worked, it made me dizzy and provided some necessary relief. With you in the air with an escort and some allies; my life has once again become the thing that Tom Clancy movies starring me and my friends are written about. Safety has become an issue again this time at a really serious level. I get truly upset like tonight worrying about it. People I love and need at the highest levels and my abilities at tapping into the brains and energy of the world as I do is very draining. The noise level inside my head is currently deafening on a world wide scale. For months I have been amping up; without trying to be able to really tune in. Apparently to be applied right now. I have something to contribute and even if I did not want to participate it lands in my lap...

So here I am this night with you... running again, flanked by more Kevlar than anyone should ever have to wear. You are hunting high threat level scumbags around the globe. Like Indiana Jones, bounty hunter, you appear. Then finally we are almost sane and you are asleep in a military bed surrounded by guns and planes and missiles safe as a bug in a rug after 3 whole weeks of being anything but. I have heard two nights of extreme primal panic in the dark marred by foreign languages and threats of a terminal nature. This kind of fear I have felt before... most people don't even know it exists. Thank God for them; blissful ignorance. They are the kind of happy that allows a normal life and happiness without any real mental maintenance or malady what- so- ever. They watch the news and 30 Rock and everything is just fine here and "out there." They take safety for granted, they are clueless... they think it just happens, kumbaya. I wish the world really was a sweet peaceful John Lennon song... but sadly no, it's not. Not then and much less now than ever before. Here's to it, closed eyes and wishful thinking, lucky them. Meanwhile, I'm tied to the other end of a phone. Grasping at every breath like straws not wanting to let you go out of complete and utter fear. Pacing wide eyed, sheet white and brain dead; waiting for that communiqué to let me know that everyone and especially you; are in one solid piece … still.

Safe and sound the way all of you were when you were all sent off in love and innocence by your families. I have communicated those nights with you all the while praying that I was partially responsible for pulling you through alive and intact.; because I helped make you clear headed and able to focus. It's vain of me to think of myself as so important to you in dire straights, but you tell me that I am. I'm young and stupid enough to believe what I hear I guess. You told me that "You are and have been my lifeline, pulling me through." "You know that I could not have done it without you helping me." I hope that I always can steer and make you hear me when you need to. I get to "hear you" by text inside a jet being whisked away like a Faberge Egg. Just so you know one of my nicknames because of a boyfriend, was always Faberge. One of his ex girlfriends met me, assumed I was a vacant, beautiful thing and that was what she nicknamed me. Now it's function is apparent. Just a typical day in my world and not surprisingly in yours as well. The precious egg head that carries all of the world in her / his insides. No one really has any idea of what's in there. They thought it was all about the luscious cover that glistens in the sunlight. But they never know about the inside which has everything to do with being able to see in the dark. Here's hoping you've become adept with your night vision glasses, I have a feeling that your gonna need them.

I hope the people around you know what they are doing and are infallible every single time, I cannot afford for them not to be. There are people I know and love, most precious cargo at stake. In all sorts of unreal and unbelievable circumstances. I have been grateful for your group and others for our safety for years, even before I met you. I understand what this means you don't need to tell me. No one is allowed anyway, I know this. I understand before it happens, I know it before it goes down, it's exhausting. To be so aware of a world you cannot see. That aside…what were the chances…really? That we would meet and that we always get out? This time, any time?

Months ago he told her "that she stepped through a dark portal and that there was no going back, ever." To her the funny part was that he thought she didn't know and that he had to tell her. Funnier still, was that he was the one along with his team that came through a numinous hole and they never knew that they did. They didn't even know that it was like "Alice Through The Looking Glass", but no one had to take a pill. It just was… all real and three dimensional every-day. "What are the chances that things could go badly?" "That things could implode?" These are the questions I ask myself every day, every time it dawns on me I dare not ask him; scared that there might be a real statistic, a number, a study or any other input that tells me that I'm correct. I don't want to be. I almost never want to be.

I found the hotel, it dropped into my lap like rain. It had a history. Only we didn't. I got an email followed a banner ad, did the research and before long we were set. I was coming to Washington and amazingly so was he after having returned from Europe, the Middle East, and other points in The Med and the Ottoman Empire. He was whole, which was unbelievable after the three weeks we had just been through in the dark on the phone in more time zones than you could count.

He continued to lie to her, as he was taught to. To protect, to save, to serve all the things that he had come into contact with up to this point in his life. The group doesn't hand you a manual on how to deal with a civilian that thinks like a high level operative, has the skill set to back it up and can move situations with her mind. This was Penn's guaranteed holy shit moment on a cracker. He let her know that he missed her while he was abroad working. He let her know that he never ached for anyone the way he ached for her. More than anything he let her know that he was intrigued, confused, scared and falling in love.

Aria, had an agenda and Penn was not prepared to deal with someone capable of loving him unconditionally. He was used to the drill...females like they are to so many of the guys in the groups are basically the enemy. They are used for sex as long as they are willing. They are collateral damage. What she was offering was called love and slowly he got the message starting on that hot summer day in the hotel that would become their place. A day with the curtains pulled, that turned into night.

She could share the driver's seat and would care for him and not hurt him. Unlike most girls that wanted to get near him, she actually was never a threat. She was head over heels in love with this man and had wanted to be with him physically, mentally and emotionally since the first ten minutes in his presence. She fell for him with complete devotion. She kept him steady and straight and he felt new found power and clarity and energy and had no idea why.

Penn was in a terrible situation in ten different places in less that two weeks, running for his life. People were trying to sabotage and kill him at every turn. Aria told her mother who knew her very intimately, that this man was speaking to her while traveling, like others had done before. That this man needed her and she could not be dragged from his side no matter what. She knew the difference between his survival and his demise and that she was standing in the way of point blank range and would not allow it to happen. Her mother was only taken aback by the profundity and the matter of fact nature of her delivery as if this happened everyday.

Grace had guarded her daughter ad nauseam for her entire life knowing what she was capable of. Quietly, never speaking about it except to tell her to not tell anyone. Never making her feel like a freak that she could do things that other people could not. The child had always been a numinous, and her mother was always afraid that there would be a knock at the door and the feds would come and take the baby away and cut her up into tiny little pieces trying to figure out why her wiring allowed her to know about things, places and people that normal people were not supposed to know. Aria was a freak, however she had always been one so with no other frame of reference she was good. No mental malady and she had serious backbone. Adversity coupled with her character had made Aria very strong. So when she met her physical, mental and emotional match she latched on in way she didn't recognize previously. There was nothing else to do other than to show him, defend, preserve and protect him. She would empower him, align him with all the power that she could move to ensure that his safety and best intentions for the world were never ever messed with. It was plain and simple just like her, her MO never changed from the time she was a child. She realized that Penn's never had either. It was one of the main issues that bonded them. A crystal clear vision of morality, of what it took.

They were like children in adult bodies, unlike most of the world which seemed to be caught in a perpetual state of teenage self absorption and entitlement. Penn and Aria were adults willing to step up and make nasty, difficult and unpopular decisions and stand by them. Responsibility is a dirty word. The difficult path represents real belief and hope for the future and people who come along long after we leave. Slogging through blood and guts now ensures stability later. Self sacrifice for people you will never know represents the ultimate in respect, honesty and love. It's not pretty but it is selfless which is immensely loving. You don't care who gets the credit. You care about the outcome, how you get there and that you do. No one does anything they do because they want to be recognized. In fact it's not in anyone's best interest to be recognized. It would compromise the process, the job and everyone's safety. And that's not an option, not today, not ever. That is our world, everyday.

Penn always dressed well, he had a penchant for conservative, classic, expensive looking casual clothing. The kind that almost smelled like money like so many other men in his profession. Clothing that would allow you to disappear in Washington, allow you to blend. There was a disparity. Some things he would spend money on; he was a total snob and other things would not even dawn on him. It had nothing to do with money.

There was always enough of that when he needed something. It had more to do with the way he was raised and the time he had been raised in. He was a punk kid, in the times everyone else was listening to The Doors and Janice and getting high. He was busy chasing girls, going to school and running with his friends while he listened to music. He would rather screw girls, play football and workout rather than get high. God forbid you would get so obliterated that you couldn't fuck well. That was so much more fun and profitable and laughable. Why would you want to get so messed up that you couldn't take care of the flavor of the week? Priorities man…where are your priorities?

With his style, he could pretend to fit in just a little bit in DC. Hell, there he was almost cutting edge. Washington was hardly a bastion of the fashion forward or for that matter of people with any awareness what so ever. Given the gay populous that alone is an oddity. Washington should be like San Francisco, NYC or Key West but it missed the memo somehow that gay men are the designated design gods. People in Washington wear their pants too high up and high waters are commonplace. From a fashion perspective and a gay one it's like a terrible accident, you can't look away. It's as if they are "Friends of Noah" instead of "Friends of Dorothy." I would shoot a picture for the paper if I ever saw a fabulous woman walking into a NOW meeting in ruby red slippers, instead of comfortable shoes.

In Washington there are only two groups that are highly divergent and both try too hard. The call girls & strippers and the Capital Hill Barbie's and all three groups are blowing a congress person and everyone knows it. Despite all of them throwing themselves at Penn he never went for it. Sure he'd gone along to the clubs… everyone in Washington uses them for meetings like Kleenex. But he always viewed those girls as exactly what they were, sales people. He didn't date down or even screw down. Most of the boys did. The boys didn't care were they put it, as long as they got it wet, they

13

were good. But as time went on Penn's whoring around started to get boring and old. Not that he would ever say this to any of his colleagues. They were single and married, younger and older, white and black and from all over the world, but they all had that one thing in common. They talked about chicks behind closed doors when they got together. The last one, the current one, the wife and her sister, the one in every port. Why they are divorcing their wife. She never ever even knew what they did. They never ever do. It was like the upper level mob but the women were dumber. The guys all did it, all the time, every day. It was their attempt at male bonding. Keeping the whores and the strippers and the lobbyists and flight attendants that weren't banging senator what's his bucket busy. They did it. They all did it. But he didn't.

Penn considered those women low end, but he wouldn't treat them poorly any day. He just wasn't buying what they were selling; he needed and wanted more. He was a true romantic. He still believed that love happened in the world, even though he'd felt that he had made bad choices and had never forgiven himself for the fact that he felt he messed up and his mom and dad would never live to see how well he'd done. That he really could love someone out there that was capable of really loving him. That contrary to what so many people had surmised he was deep, passionate and a soft touch. A serious contradiction to the job he did every day. Still no one knew, except her. She knew. She knew about him and about his life from the very first moment she laid eyes on him. And it still scared the crap out of him every single day.

Penn couldn't put his finger on what was so horrifying that very first day or week. He just jumped on that plane to the Med with a picture of a girl in his minds eye. That one afternoon meeting changed his point of view and things would never be the same. She started to talk to him while he was in the Med, after many days of doing most of the listening. He dissected every word she said and wrote them all down. Aria met Penn and suddenly she thought about things she had never wanted before. She looked at families when they were out together. She looked at couples, young married happy people and older happy married people and wondered how they did it. Wondered why it was them and not her. Not her and this specific man sitting across from her; that she could no longer survive without the scent of him on her clothes.

All of this discourse and banter on the phone and in their heads and they didn't even take into account the number of people in the big room that were listening live by satellite. Virtually guaranteeing that everyone on the team would know about all of the strangeness of this interaction after a short period of time. That the odd pairing would be a topic of conversation in the covert marble halls, with only the highest level of clearance. Aria had been avoiding being drafted or participating with the group for a few years now and was quite proud that she managed to stay out of the web this long. Knowing she would get no support from her family and would be sent to some far flung address abroad. Aria knew, it was just never talked about. When friends and family are highly involved, it just sort of is. You never really think or know anything different. So Aria had the beginnings of a life and it was truly strange and colorful and then she met an unlikely compatriot who stole her heart and then she went to get her gun to cover him. This was a pretty strong reaction for someone who had never defended anyone who wasn't a blood relative before. People did not just pass through her life, she felt them. Penn wondered for a while why Aria didn't like women very much, and then he finally understood their typical pattern of behavior, he got it. Because of the way she looked, women treated her terribly everywhere she went, all day long everyday. It became annoying to him, because Aria was good to everyone and she had no agenda, so to constantly watch her being treated poorly was exhausting and it hurt him deeply.

Aria let him know about most women, that you could not trust them at all. "If men tried to get away with what women do by nature they would all kill each other and never have one single friend." Her typical play was men of all ages would be shot down if they came in too close at range, she was rarely impressed. It was almost

15

never worth the effort or the heartbreak. Learning that your guy was more comfortable in your skirt than you was never fun and waxed eyebrows were a non starter. Her standards, unlike a guys general MO (barely breathing) were like Everest. Good luck with that was a typical level of inner dialogue for her.

CHAPTER THREE

She knew what he did and had absolutely no problem with any of it. She could do it herself. She was a hard ass. At least that's what people thought she was, because the people who knew her well, understood that she could do that job and sleep like a baby at night, just like he did. The jobs that no one else wanted to do. The forward movement; the attention to detail and a specific MO. The gathering of information and the occasional assassination of someone, anyone, a world leader when necessary to save a larger group of people. To save all the kids at soccer games and kids having their first beer, or sex or baby. So that people would be around to do good for the world. To make sure that they actually got the option. She knew all of it. That he killed people for a living. Only when they needed killing. Sometimes people do.

Sometimes people just need to get kicked out of the gene pool. When they chose the option of peeing in the pool, and that was unacceptable no matter what the reason. Because everyone has to swim in the water. This was an issue that they agreed on to the extreme. These were some of uncomfortable adult decisions that small elite groups of people around the globe were saddled with making, daily. The kinds of things that the teenagers running around shooting their mouths off about in social media out of ignorance will never know. They think they have the real input, but to be honest there are too many pieces in motion and they don't have the real details anyway.

They are the new Michael Moore's and Oliver Stones. They have no idea that there are groups planning their and their children's and their dog's demise daily. They rebuke the very free system that has provided for their families. They think they are going to sit around a tent and make smores, speak in altiloquent tones and sing songs and blog about their graham crackers and pop tarts, but they aren't. The people that we are dealing with are survivalists with nothing to lose to the extreme and they don't eat fucking smores or give a shit that you do. The truth of the life on this planet at times more often than not outside of this and a few select zip codes is quite ugly. Of course when their sister's A train blows up on her way to her Times internship they will be the first person to lawyer up and sue the city and say why me?

As for him because of survival for life in the field he was built big, and I mean physically large. She never liked or even looked at men like that before but now he did it for her. He made her feel safe. One day in a hotel in Washington that was crawling with alphabet agents of every kind, she was sitting in the basement, in a chair after a crazy fire drill for no reason. A ridiculously well built clone of her man was painfully aware of her sitting in the corner, but she never gave him the time of day.

For Aria the grey matter was everything and it was non negotiable. It was the only thing that kept her around and interested. Sex, when someone liked it, could be taught. Someone could be built in to an effective lover; they could not however be taught to be highly intelligent and then have the kinds of conversations that those people have. They could not accumulate that time in the field, process it and survive the way that the best, brightest and luckiest do. There was no substitute for pure excellence and she knew it. He had been given a number since she had known him. Shortly after they met. She was there when it went down. At that exact moment, they knew where she was and what they were doing... the agencies were already watching her anyway. They knew that she knew what they were up to, surprisingly. She had already been told that "Her credibility had already been widely established." "Bonus" Aria thought to herself.

Which is agency hierarchy BS for carry on we're okay with you, we know you're a good person and we have every intention of tapping you when we need to... don't be alarmed. She was well aware of the fact that she had been used as a diversion somewhere in the beginning, and then things went horribly wrong. They started to care about her. Her openness and fearless devotion to the man she loved was measurable, palpable. It affected people and things at the agency and events that he was supposed to attend with her as a beautiful distraction on his arm providing him and her and the group with a more well supported cover and a serious illusion–suddenly didn't.

People that he had been told that were okay to trust during operations, she told everyone in the big room were not okay. This did not make everyone very happy. The fact of the matter was that, she was right and they were wrong. Things proved to be worse than that on many occasions and Aria was almost always right. When this happened and everyone could see proof of her abilities, things were definitely not okay. Aria became an asset to the asset, and this was a new position for everyone at the party and suddenly nobody felt like dancing. Times like these made large groups of people uncomfortable, first and foremost they made Aria and Penn uncomfortable because for the first time they became aware that their privacy was a thing of the past.

After a while Penn and Aria began to speak normally while he was in the field, because they just didn't care anymore. It was too much bullshit to play charades anyway. It got to the point where they would have had phone sex from the field, from far flung foxholes in Karachi and in Paris hotels just to make it reverberate around Langley in the big room in stereo. They took great pleasure in making even the most callous operatives blush like an eleven year old. That game was always a nice distraction when his ass was on the line in some foreign, sandy, shithole with the cockroaches breathing down his neck. They both traveled constantly, so until they could be together permanently their life took place in hotels. Hotels, all over the world were viewed as home and had come to represent, happiness, normalcy, comfort and safety. Of course they weren't really any of those things and in the back of their minds sadly they knew it. They suppressed it, the sadness of the situation, until they could make it different. Anyone with a normal and boring life would have thought that their situation was wildly exciting, sexy and romantic. But what this high powered couple wanted worse than anything in the world was a break. To be left alone in a safe place where no one on the planet knew where they were, there was no GPS, where the phone would not ring and where the only people with weapons and a license to use them effectively were them.

They wanted it, longed for it, prayed for it, talked about it. They were doing everything that they could to make it a reality sooner rather than later. At one point they were ready to live on government property in a house if everyone agreed to leave them the fuck alone for a few weeks.

There had been more than a few physical maladies accumulated in Penn's personal life, and in the field in the past year, and Penn had been given almost no down time to have multiple surgeries and repairs to his body. He having been dispatched to multiple hostile third world and other situations while trying to recover. This gave Aria an ulcer of course and her new found relationship with her digestive tract was legendary. It became so crazy for awhile that almost every time he went out he would get shot. Not shot at, that was a given, but shot. Then there were the more superficial wounds that could always be counted on, shrapnel spray, hyper extended ligaments and cuts, broken bones and severe disturbing bacterial infections.

Aria always knew about the dangers Penn would face before they happened... the details in her mind's eye were staggering and they constantly blew Penn's mind. They both got to the point where they would take notes and compare them down to the minute after the ops, sometimes as much as four weeks later but it was always more than a little horrifying how deadly accurate down to the minute she was about his state of affairs.

As if she was standing in the room; from all the way across the world. From his point of view. With no details, no contact or input. She was balls on. She was the human Garmin. It still unnerved him, even after a year. But after a while he came to accept that he was in love with someone that no one was built to understand except the few others that roamed the planet that had similar capabilities.

It took awhile to identify issues and there were specific people who dealt with the problems that were unique to life inside, outside and adjacent to the agency and any and all of the alphabet agencies. It was a crazy life and not something that someone should be expected to cope with on their own. Aria was acutely aware of this fact. Sometimes you needed a little help, to blow off some steam and spending it with someone you consider a friend that you can trust sounded vastly superior to going full postal and doing something in life or in the field that's hard to undo. You don't want to go there, ever. It's not like you can be part of the deal and just speak to anyone on the outside about anything anyway. Even a serious doctor, for starters they would think you were bat shit crazy. Then if they did ever believe that you were for real, one of two things would ensue.

They would either tell their colleagues, feeling that they actually have a crazy patient. Then you would have a group that knew about your opps. Oh boy! Or if they really believed you, then they would think you were a dangerous psychopath and call the cops. That would be even worse because then papers would be filed, pictures would be taken and covers would be blown and that would suck, badly. With that in mind, there was a shrink that they found in order to help them cope. She started the relationship to deal with the extreme stress, and after many months pulled Penn in.

Doc Minor became family, he was a safe place in a unsafe situation. The Doc was wonderful and elflike and open and pure. He was such an anomaly in the group in so many ways. He was relaxed and open and figured her out immediately. They became fast friends, first Aria and Doc Minor and then the three of them. When it was time to do any kind of evaluation, he was the guy from the very beginning. The rule was this, at some point you just know too much crazy stuff and it had to be kept in check. Downloaded, as it were, kept in a safe and controlled environment with air–conditioning and motion sensors to make everyone happy and to keep it cool ... This is what Doc's first function was, climate controlled safe, hand carry storage.

This was convenient because Penn and Aria both had a anger management problem and a high boiling point. When they both got riled up it would get loud and confrontational but not with each other. There they were gentle as lambs, there they came to count on each other to calm down. This behavior first reared it's head in Washington at a hotel clerk. When Aria shooshed Penn, and shot him a "stop it baby" look. Penn was over- reacting because he was upset about something else that had happened to Aria moments before. It had absolutely nothing to do with the dumb, inept, snotty girl behind the desk. She was just some bitch in the way.

CHAPTERFOUR

Penn woke up in a cold sweat again, for where he was you would think that it would finally be getting cooler, and of course he wasn't on the ground floor in this hotel. Never on the ground floor, ever. Unless it was a setup, with home court advantage and friends. This was nobody's home court. It was the middle of the night and even with what precious little sleep he got, he was awake again, he'd been dreaming about home and hearth and what life would be like with her, and it jarred him more than the shithole he'd been sent to for at least a week. Karachi was not his favorite place so as fate would have it, the location for his latest assignment and his current base of operations. Murphy's Law, scumbag central. Pakistan is like Atlanta's Hartsfield airport or Frankfurt airport in Germany but for terrorists; all things must past through Pakistan. It's like terrorist Disneyland.

Penn was good, he was so good that he could tell you about people walking down the street; their region of the world even if they were in Ohio. He described them as having big red arrows over their heads as if there were signs telling you what country and region they hailed from. Like balloons in comic strips so patently clear. These were not things that he was taught, these were things that he learned because of time tested blood and sweat on the ground, up to his ass in survival.

"When we catch a terrorist–we find creative ways to extract information; and when someone breaks they tell you all sorts of valuable intel about their movements who does what where and with whom." But the one thing that you can always count on is that there will always, and I mean always, be a floor bob of the head to Karachi and or Islamabad and they'll talk about it like they speak about martyrdom, psychotically, lovingly, glowingly. "Gee Hamid, now that you've been charged with your orders for eternity what are you going to do?" "I'm going to Disneyland... I mean Pakistan!" the boy exclaimed. Pakistan is like Wal-Mart for terrorists, one stop shopping. They don't care where the shit comes from, there's always a buyer and a seller and everyone is willing to undercut anyone from anywhere. They all run through the turnstiles knowing that it will be easy and that everyone will be at the party. No one ever guards the door or mans the velvet rope or checks the invites or the list, there's not even a doorman to be paid off; that would be Saudi Arabia. As crappy as the set up is, this makes Pakistan on any given day spy central. A mix of locals, good guys, extreme bad guys and worse bad guys passing through from all over. It's a shithole, in a shitstorm in the middle of a sand–storm, with lousy food and a bad attitude. Welcome to Pakistan, enjoy your stay. No wonder so many people are pissed off and are trying to leave any way they can. It's like Tijuana on crack times ten.

To attempt to blend in as a white or black agent is a thing to behold and not an easy trick at that. Taller, heavier, healthier and whiter makes for being easily marked on the street. A big no- no and a serious non starter, it's dangerous to your well being and your ability to move about freely. To get in and out when you have to, with who and or what you came for. The only time this is a positive thing, is when you run across a friendly, one of ours or an Israeli. This in those special situations, will save your red, white and blue American ass. Of course agents have to be judged on a case by case basis, and you can find good people anywhere. They exist all over in all countries, they are all colors and religions and they are all ages. Sometimes in the places that you would least expect. Sometimes the worst ones and the people you cannot trust are your own, Penn thought. "Just look at that fool down at Ft. Hood. Political correctness was responsible for many deaths and that guy never should have been in the position to do such harm." Tipping his hand months before on multiple occasions in front of other officers etc. Then he was promoted to major in March after multiple reprimands. Sent to colleges to take courses on his chosen faith and radical behavior. "What's the deal with that?" Yelled Penn in his own head. "Exactly who the hell was minding the store here?" "Not to mention he was caring for stressed people coming and going from the field. A place he had never even been... really... come on."

But because of his ethnic background, despite his unhinged belief system, they never got rid of him. They should have canned him the minute that he showed he was mentally unstable. The White House just needs to leave the alphabet agencies which risk their lives everyday the hell alone, period. So that we are not sending mixed messages to people who would discipline and bounce out people who are chock full of crazy, radical, risky, detrimental behavior. Profiling is not a bad thing even if people do not like it, it works. Boo Frickin Hoo, deal with it America. Do you understand the way the rest of the world really works here? Point in fact–you believe the news and you don't have the real information and you're not going to get it anytime soon, and most of you could not handle it anyway. Hell, right now 1600 can't handle it. There are at last count, twelve families that have been robbed of vital members of their clan because someone was worried about how it would look and what everyone would think if someone cried wolf. That is so much like a third grader. What if they don't like me, whine. Who gives a damn, do you think those people who died give a shit who liked them? Hell no, they would rather be alive; the bad guy is alive, while valuable beings, loving people, good people met their maker at his evil ass hand.

This discovery of good people in different situations had of course become readily apparent to Penn more than once over twenty years. And he has worked with groups of people from many countries who have surprisingly not let him down, despite terrible circumstances, they have done their jobs and risen to the occasion.

Being able to speak some semblance of Arabic has also helped a lot, given the circumstances. But Pakistan is a place that you come to that knowing before you leave, if you do, that there will be at least one group, or person of some sort, whose main objective is to kill you. Your job is to do the same to them, and not be on the receiving end. Plain and simple. Oh, and then of course it's your job is to get out, alive and intact. Preferably the way you came in, so the illusion is complete and that you can one day return to do something similar. However, the people chasing you on this or any other day while on your way to successfully complete this operation are not so convinced that letting you get through customs and on to that plane is such a great idea. You see they had other plans for your day and will now probably lose their hands and, or heads to their superiors because they screwed up and let you get away, again. No wonder they hate you, because it sucks to be them. Losing your head is detrimental to your health and it hurts, a lot.

There were already some countries that were off limits to Penn entirely. They would be left for others to tend to. They were just too dangerous for him to ever go back. He would be a marked man the minute he cleared customs. In fact, he would never even see the outside of the airport, it was that bad. But most people never knew how bad it actually was. Surely civilians home safe and sound in the States never got the memo; that things were out of control while they went to the drive through and got their designer coffee and NY Times. They spent their time reading about how we won't deal with Darfur or illegal immigrants. They were super busy making sure everyone got free health care and college and that they got their asses kissed. They were anticipating getting read a story at bed time. They were busy, making sure that pets could sue their owners over how big bad and capitalistic America was, just in general.

He was over it, waking up in Karachi after a few hours of sleep and clearing passport control. He was due at his first meeting within a couple of hours and he had to get up, get a shower, find food and potable water and check in with a secure up link, all before lunch. It was going to be a full and long day and God only knows what it would bring.

For all the prep you did and all the pre field briefs, years of experience had shown him that being a spy and being a successful trial lawyer were close bed fellows. No matter how much you did, how much you prepared things, everything was always was more complex and always went awry and got out of control at the absolute worst most compromising time. Then you had to pull rabbits out of your ass in a foreign, hostile land and make it work at all costs or you would not be going home to see your kids. Point blank range. That was where the problems always surfaced, at point blank range. In your face and then they had to be dealt with. There was no pussy footing around. It was never pretty and people regularly made unscheduled exits. It was always big and crucial and you're far from home and quite fucked... so you had better be connected, confident and callous to any anarchy that may ensue because you have to really think on your feet. That ability to think on your feet and that gnaw in your gut most of the time, will be what in all honesty saves your life in some foreign third world shithole. He thanked God for his ability at the cellular level to know the difference daily. That specific ability had put his happy ass, post op, back in a debriefing situation both home and abroad for many years. Easier said than done always.

He thought about it while staring at the ceiling waking up. What makes a great agent and not just simply a good one, a competent one? One who keeps coming back alive? What makes an expert? What were the common qualities? Did he posses any of those qualities? Did the agency have a list with boxes that got ticked off? How many boxes had been checked next to his name? Agggh! There was too much to think about this early and he needed to find some Evian and brush his teeth and take a piss. He had been too tired when he arrived to even pee. The time difference always killed you for the first few days and he would be staying up later than he should to call back to the East coast to talk to her at a time he felt he would not tip his hand. Plus he had to lie about where he was and that required the quiet of the dead of night in Pakistan and no mosques in the background blaring their calls to prayer. He had no clue that she already knew where he was and what he was doing anyway. He was back in the Middle East and the Far Eastern region and his body and soul was none the worse for the wear... amazing. That was something neither he nor the agencies officers could say about most of their agents or the lifers at his level. He used to say that he was good at his job and to him he was stating a fact to make other people feel better. It was never a statement of ego, it was designed to make other people feel more comfortable, that's all. It was a highly accurate statement and given his boy scout bent, you could see he was convincing himself every time he uttered it.

As time went on and multiple trips to Pakistan ensued Aria became emboldened because like the terrorists she had an end game, his well being. She knew the situations would amp up over the many months and she began to shoot her mouth off to him in private as well as in the big room many times so the home office would know that she understood .

Penn had seen so many people come and go and not come home over the years or crack up completely that he was more than slightly amused that he had been such a lucky bastard. All of this work through the years had given him many specialties that he would come to be known for around Langley. Penn was like a bird for one thing, like a human carrier pigeon on several levels and continents for better or for worse. The ways he managed to move material both physical things and his mental capacity was legendary. He was humble and played the bumbling superman, everyman quite literally. On his last assignment he carried a gift for Aria out across the border between his formidably sized testicles. He thought nothing of it. "Keep all the precious cargo in one place" it made perfect sense to Penn. He left the gift in his office as he left in a hurry. Though he quickly told her that he forgot it upon seeing her at their rendezvous post operation. He felt terrible and wanted to wanted to bring it to her next time he saw her. Aria was flattered, and was sure that this was absolutely the farthest any human being had ever gone thinking of her as to bring her a gift from behind enemy lines carried underneath the balls she worshiped on a regular basis.

He loved that about her. That she worshiped him just as much as he worshiped her and you could tell every time they were within feet of each other. He would tell her that she was like sex on a stick. She knew it, and she loved the fact that he got it. The sex was that good. He had waited his whole life for this kind of relationship with the whole package as he liked to call her. He said that their physical relationship was better than porn. All this and brains too. Long before they got involved during his trip to the Med, he started quizzing her about sex. He knew he was more than interested and slowly she started to answer specific queries. He was surprised, so much so that he thought she must be lying. But as time went on he got to know her and over many months he learned that she rarely had the patience to lie, unlike most people. She just didn't bother. She really didn't care what most people thought about her enough to lie, in order to advance her placement in anything. It was a conscious choice. She had bigger balls than most men, hell than most agents. She was damn near fearless across the board and that was scary as all get out. Damn her, he loved it that she didn't need him, she wanted him. Needing him came much later and he was grateful when it finally did, when he could feel it. When the day came that he knew beyond the shadow of a doubt that she loved him, he understood his place in the universe once again, and it made him at times feel exhausted and invincible.

CHAPTERFIVE

On the beginnings of this field trip out Reagan was teeming. Teeming with People and Spies, commuting Lobbyists, Journalists, Capital Hill Barbies and Senators, all things Washington. Reagan is under so much surveillance because of it's history that it feels like a Vegas casino or a cruise ship to all points. Every God damned moment is video taped. The video tape is video taped, it's insane. It was like a great agent, it only pretends to miss a trick. The trick is… is that it never ever does. Every once in a while somewhere in the world you would see someone that you know or that you have worked with, shared moments with and it's always weird. You're not allowed to acknowledge or interact; so there's always that grey area when you come upon someone. It had happened to him a few times, sometimes at airports.

He always thought about that…she knew pretty much everything. This day and every day while he tried to ready himself in his hotel room, a world away inside his head. "While I'm Sitting at Reagan waiting to go… it's fascinating and horrifying all at the same time, it's a "Capital Hill Petrie Dish." Biological soup for operatives the world over." It all just hurt her head. She was tapping into him as usual and her thoughts flew back and fourth between what Penn was experiencing and what was happening in front of her like a tennis match. Aria watched agents mingling with the regular folks. To her it felt like a sideshow at a county fair. See the foreign operative swallow a sword and eat fire.

She could almost always make every operative encountered. Sometimes she would only have to hear someone's name or hear them speak and she knew their true identity. "I'm one of the only people sitting here that no one could figure out what I actually do, guaranteed." "Most of the people here would peg me quite incorrectly; what they wouldn't get is that I'd be the first to pack off to whatever land with a weapon inside a body part with the flag tattooed on my ass ... Just call me Rip Van Winkle, wake me when it's over. Are we there yet?"

While buzzing around his hotel room with all this live in his head Penn was not yet aware of how much Aria hated certain countries because she understood how the governments operated in less than democratic circumstances. She also worried because she always knew where he would be going to work before he did. She always had site specific information on how it would go down. That was the terrible thing for her, always knowing in advance and then having to deal with the management and acceptance of the information in her own head no matter what it was.

Only days before this field trip to Pakistan had started with Penn trying to break up with her when he was overwhelmed. Aria didn't walk away when he tried to come back. That was how their Thanksgiving holiday started. "You're being dumped, I'm freaking out and I'm going to Pakistan as chum to try and get killed, pass the white meat please."

Aria got weak in the knees and wanted to vomit but she swallowed hard and the vomit came out as tears instead. She felt she would for the first time die without him. She was in Miami Airport standing over the design of hurricane Andrew at the time. She was really in Miami for that too. Aria laughed when she thought about that day and all the experiences that they managed to cram into a matter of weeks and months and how intense and serious things had become in their life together. It blew her mind constantly. Before they were sitting in this weeks selection of countries, hotels and multiple airports; there had been some discussions about their predicaments and the constant threat of blood–letting being taken as a given. Aria confronted him with the what if's and the problems. It was like making a will. That conversation made both of them very uncomfortable, but it had to be done. After all he said he wanted to spend the rest of his life with her. That he couldn't and didn't want to live without her and his goal for starters was to marry her. Or rather to get her to agree to marry him. He knew that would be a tall order and he thought about it every hour of every day. His life had become a chick flick and for the first time he didn't mind. This chick was no estrogen laden bitch, she was a super hero with a heart and soul and big brass ovaries that clanged together when she shimmied her heart shaped ass across a room, just like his balls. It was a brand new day. He made sure that the top brass knew it all. That unlike the usual deal, this was not just some mind blowing "POA" Piece Of Ass. This girl was in for the long haul. That she was his touchstone and point of contact for the world and the only person that truly knew him and that he was grateful that he found her at all. He never thought he would. They were to speak only with Aria. He would tell her from the field that if "I died right now I would die a happy man because for the first time in my life I know who I love, and who loves me. I have waited my whole life up to this point for you. I did not think that you existed. I am devastated everyday that my mother and father are gone, and that they will never meet or know you. That I had my children with someone else, though I love them very much. I have met the person that I was always supposed to be with, my soul mate." Once Penn arrived at that point he never looked back. Aria made it clear to him that she would be the one reaching out to his girls, should things go terribly wrong. That she would make sure that they came to a place of love and understanding about the man that they and their mother really did not know at all. The man that spent time away from the time that they were small, defending the world and all the good peace loving people in it. Maybe if he worked hard by the time that they were adults, there might still be a world for them to participate in. That's what he was shooting for anyway. A place for them to have their own lives, dogs and maybe even husbands and babies.

Sadly, Penn's wife and he were better apart than together. They had already made a pact to stay together only for the children; so he was gone a great deal. He went abroad regularly, flying all over the world and he took many types of transportation. This travel time was useful on many levels, Penn's self awareness and internal knowledge would reach new highs over the next year. He let the brass know that "if anything happened to him that they would be lucky if Aria agreed to even be recruited." That would be the only thing that might garner a yes on her part. Aria had already fed the group so much valuable information. More than he had time to follow up on. So he just kicked it up the ladder. Aria was valid and everyone was beginning to know it. They were the most effective and unique unit on the planet with capabilities together that no on else had. The group got the message and decided it would be better to saddle this horse, take the reigns, direct the head and ride than to not have control at all.

Penn had managed his uplink with little difficultly after climbing out of the shower, and he hoped that this would be the measure of the day. Getting last minute phone calls from Langley always perked up his ears. At least today there would only be phone calls to one place and he would not have to call and tease his "Mama Bear". Mama Bear is what Penn called the "den mother" for his unit that kept tabs on him the world over, so that more than one person of trust knew his movements.

He checked in often and would catch reprimands when he did not. The group was very serious about the safety of their agents / assets. When he was on an op all of those groups held hands immediately, so Mama Bear would not have the pleasure of getting grief from her favorite agent today. Secretly, Penn missed talking to his Mama Bear, she was a ritual of life for many years and to change the rhythm always was strange. Today had not been harsh or unexpected from his point of view. Just some last minute operational details, updates, nothing crazy or out of left field.

Thank God for small favors, he had too much on his mind already and for Christ sakes he woke up after three hours of sleep in Pakistan. Things don't really get any stranger than that. He just got there and already he hated it. The smell was like a camel's ass, it was hideous. The noise of the people just functioning. The pallor of blue grey smog that hangs over the city constantly, so that between that and the dust you could never stay clean for even half the day. The terrible smell of the people everywhere. In the States we were so spoiled, we were obsessed with cleanliness. The constant in your face poverty here was oppressive. The worst were the children, orphans starving, neglected and abused everywhere. The way the men treated the women as chattel and non persons… and how Islam condoned it, every bit.

He couldn't wait to get the fuck out. Penn was already counting the minutes in the days. Hoping that the whole operation went picture perfect and he could get on a plane to the next location as soon as possible and that would be that. If he ended up in a place where Islam was not the rule of the day next it would be easier to call the girl, even if someone was chasing his ass. The God damn mosque announcements were loud as all hell, and he could not risk having that shit in the back round of a casual phone call to someone having a normal day. She was smart, really smart and she would have gotten it and traced it by sound and figured it all out and that he could not afford. Plus Langley would have been pissed at his carelessness anyway. So that was it. Today was going to be text message heavy, no calls, lalalallllla over the loud speakers hanging off the turrets a zillion times a day, stuck in Pakistan, oh joy.

Off to his first meeting hitting the street. Trying to blend, walking slumped to appear shorter and less physically formidable. Drab colors, cheaper clothes than he liked. Work clothes, not the cool spy stuff like everyone thinks you wear. Dark clothes are always best, they travel well, they don't show dirt in dusty dirty places. Most of all dark clothes don't show blood, in case you get any on you. You know that's gonna come in handy, because someone almost always gets shot. More often than not, it's what you're there to do.

It's not like there's water everywhere and you're likely to find a spy standing in his drawers and socks in someone's hotel room washing the blood out of his shirt bobbing his head to his ipod singing "I Will Survive." Never gonna happen. But you can't really be tooling around Karachi or Islamabad in a blood splattered shirt. You're trying to blend, remember jackass your white, rough trade. Don't wear or take anything you love or you will be liberated of it. It's always a cheap throw away. There are many more of them than you so you don't invite trouble. In Islamabad or Karachi trouble finds you with no map ap needed. So blend, blend, blend as much as possible. It's always a crap shoot which side wants to have you there less. Do you want to be there even less than they want you there? It's like the guy who's taking everyone's money and winning at poker. The entire time that guy is there you're plotting how to take your money back. But you don't want him to leave until you have your money back. That's why everyone gets drunk because they know they are not getting their money back. Same as why everyone joins the Jihad. Life sucks in Pakistan for most poverty stricken men and they will try to get out any way that they can; even if they have to escape to the after life in order to get laid by some chick who would never ever blow them in this life. So, as a rule, they don't have a lot to lose and they have a bad attitude and now some imam comes along and tells them in their next life their lot will be different. Damn, where do I sign up? Who do I have to kill?

That big white guy, with a big dick, a hot girlfriend and a nice car. Cool, I can do that. That Allah is one cool dude, bonus.

Aria thought his whole career description was insane but she would never tell him that until months later. She was sweating it, badly. Penn was in the Med and multiple other locations and he was being threatened. The first time they were on the phone when the shit hit the fan, was their first field trip"together." She knew he was in dire straights. She did the one thing that should have given her abilities away. She dropped "the F bomb" live in the big room, via satellite. She was not in the habit of swearing especially in front of people, and never that word. Hell or damn sure, but not fuck! She knew he was in trouble one afternoon, and she yelled FUCK! loudly during one of their heated conversations. She wanted him out of there. She was mortified, she apologized profusely and it bothered her for months. She told him she knew everyone and their mother heard her. She was so embarrassed, she wanted to crawl into a hole. Penn told her what she already knew, that they were used to it. "Hell, you should hear us." I guess no one ever says "oh gee" on a black box, they swear like sailors under great duress, it's human nature. The group was quite familiar with behaviors like this but still it horrified her.

Sitting in a restaurant wasn't a foreign function to him and neither was ordering Middle Eastern food. What was foreign, was the waiting in a hostile country watching the door. Having placed himself in the power position in the room where he could see everything that he needed to and ID'd the other ways out of the building. The location of the bathroom, it's windows. He was as relaxed as bait could be. He was waiting… pretending to be something that he was not and following in someone else's footsteps to gather information. Months from now the valuable intel he managed to gather on this trip would give the agency the input they needed for the next go round and the ability to make some semblance of amends for wrongs that had been done to others.

Often during specific operations that are set into motion for one cause or to further one agenda, it works out that agents often scratch the back of another need, that is in fact more immediate, and critical in nature. In other words while someone is in the field out doing their job, they often trip over something (that we didn't know about) that is very valuable and unique that we are grateful to get and put to use very quickly. We like to refer to this as "a happy accident." "Happy Accidents" happen all the time and they are so valuable that our Intel agencies really could not be as effective without them. What you learn when you're on the ground for a period of time, and find yourself in reprehensible situations time and time again is this. Contrary to what Washington currently supports or the news organizations report on here there is no substitute for Intel and people on the ground and long term investment in loyal locals.

The good agents that peace loving, democratic nations inter-ject regularly to hotspots and potential hotspots around the world are amongst the bravest, most valuable, selfless beings on the planet. Most of them do not get out alive. There are in fact, very few old agents. It is a very exclusive and small club that you cannot ever admit that you were a part of. Very few people aspire to com-ing home to their families in pieces in a plastic garbage bag. But to the agents who work in this part of the world, that is a common real world scenario and an everyday reality. Something that their families will never know. Something that the current administra-tion takes for granted and for lack of experience believes that has outlived its usefulness. People pay the ultimate price often for our benefit and no one is even allowed to admit they exist.

But the teams know the cost, when they sign their lives over to every other decent citizen in the world. They make real time decisions to preserve life, limb and safety for all the people of the world, irregardless of someone's nationalistic leanings. "I see very few people currently at 1600 or staff members willing to do that" thought Penn. The world not blowing itself up is a positive thing. Things not falling into the wrong hands so that someone who is a selfish decision maker doesn't get that option are a positive thing. Most of what the agencies do are things along these lines. Very little is actually punishment for past deeds, though most involved wish it was a bigger part of it.

The good guys like to win and when someone who is good is wronged or innocents are hurt American's love to step up and level the playing field. American's were the underdogs in the beginning so they can relate to being taken advantage of and underestimated and they don't like it very much. People around the world are now looking at doing things big and small to oust oppressive, violent, abusive, corrupt regimes and looking for guidance and backup and a friend to assure them that they're doing the right thing. But as much as our people on the ground like to assist at all levels, and revel in watching colleges and hospitals and restaurants spring up in places where they used to spew hate and make weapons, it's difficult. When you're around to see people be able to pass health, safety, prosperity, a work ethic and peace on to their children that is a good day, a very good day indeed. Uniquely, we've built our whole society on good days, despite peoples different backgrounds from all four corners. We make an unwritten agreement to play by these rules. We even authored a series of documents to communicate and clarify our approach. The most important being the constitution, it is the document that does most of the heavy lifting. It's worked quite well so far.

Some of the biggest believers in that series of documents and the sanctity of them are the guys and girls on the ground. They prove it every single day by putting their selfless backsides on the line, so all of us can have a quality of life, safety and prosperity that exists in only a few places on the planet. Because many of us take what they do for granted and not having to worry about the big stuff, we get to have what we consider normal lives.

CHAPTERSIX

But back to Karachi, where he was waiting. Waiting to see what would happen, waiting to make contact. Waiting to see what he thought this day might bring. That's the thing about assignments and especially in this part of the world they were always such a crap shoot and different here than anywhere else. No matter how well executed they were on our end, no matter how well intentioned the people or the planning, they get a little funky. "They never turned out anything like the way we planned them." Sure, you might get your objectives and then some met but if you managed to stay alive and afloat and do multiple operations there the outcome was always the same. "Mitigating damage or future damage. There were just so many of them, the jihadists, so many bad guys and so many people that didn't care what or who they lost."

"Money rules the day and there were always more bad guys to slow down, interrogate, kill or track to get to a bigger fish. There were so many groups, splinter groups and subversive cells that connecting them would be akin to the human genome mapping project. Driving them was a mélange of motivations; if it wasn't money, it was hatred of the US or nationalistic fervor or religious zealotry or just a warped perspective spawned by the poverty that had doomed millions of people to a life of misery and despair around the globe. For many of these groups, recruiting young people, even children, is no problem because anything looks better than what this life has dealt them."

Among the first to sign up are the brain dead people between 12–72 that are willing to blow themselves to hell, and for what. "What a shitty testament to the state of the human condition," Penn thought every time he ventured into the Sand box or an East European Ghetto or a jungle infested with would be "revolutionaries" hell bent on targeting the US in one way or another. Fortunately, most of these human malcontents didn't have the knowledge, the goods, or the backing and the experience to carry out a successful operation. Whether it was to pull off another 9 /11, infiltrate a government R&D lab or penetrate the US intelligence community–most being the operative word. But some did. And they were getting better and they were damn persistent. The way that America naively allows these people into our country and then shields them with the very laws that were crafted to protect the peace loving Americans that they seek to destroy, blew his mind everyday.

The average person was so out of touch with the reality of the situation worldwide that it baffled those who saw what was happening every single day. Penn saw it. It tore at him and fed a seething hatred for the country's enemies and his compulsion to eliminate them whenever he could. Everyone felt the same protective urge. The Brits were so disappointed with their own past foreign policy misjudgements that they had all but begged America to learn from their naive, fantasyland approach.

France and some other countries in the EU had come to the realization that radical Islam was a cancer to be contained or excised from the country's social and political fabric. Some leaders had been stepping it up lately struggling to keep their citizens safe. But that's the reality of control when some crazy radical group has malevolent intent if you don't crush it coming through the door, you pay for it in bodies one hundred fold later. But by then it's too late to stop the snowball from going downhill and all you can do is mitigate damage which might as well be full time slavery. It's a terrible drag. The reality of the world is something that most happy go lucky Americans never acknowledged. He and other senior operatives often discussed how American foreign policy had seemingly gotten less influential with each passing year and garnered less respect around the globe. Faith in America abroad had slipped, and so had America's backers. Foreign governments in countries that were not our allies reveled, and they were all too ready to fill the vacuum, exploiting the weakness, lack of experience and no stomach for reality.

To calm himself and achieve blessed relief from his angst, he let his thoughts about the girl run wild. For the girl who had turned his own crazy world upside down, he would do anything, think about music, sex, foreign policy, his girls, his car. Living a double life was one thing, but Aria was something else. He obsessed over the girl and when they might speak again.

Later in the week, when he knew he would be in another location, he thought about the fact that he might have the chance to stop in one of his favorite local restaurants with the proverbial million dollar view. He wanted her there sitting across from him, smiling at him while the sun went down, the ruins of the Acropolis silhouetted against the sky in the distance. He pictured her there with him in a little black dress from Paris, a little bit longer than too short to conceal the palm sized pistol he knew she would have strapped to the inside of what had to be the most delicious thigh he could ever imagine kissing. He had yet to sample the real article, but he hoped to be on his way sooner rather than later. In the meantime, he indulged his wildest fantasies, which would rival anything Larry Flynt or Hugh Heffner could conjure up in their one track minds.

Penn also thought about his kids, he usually panicked just a bit whenever he got sent out on an extended assignment abroad. As his daughters had gotten older he reveled in the new found relationships he was able to have with these newly minted adults in which he had poured years of love and nurturing. He was a proud father and growing prouder every year at how the girls were maturing. However, a new kind of problem was emerging, their growing curiosity about him and the world he inhabited. They had started asking more questions.

Because of pop culture and heightened awareness, being his kids and their own smarts; they were less and less satisfied with his answers. Penn found himself torn between being a parent wanting them to use their brains to figure it out and covering his ass as an operative. It was an internal struggle that all the agents faced about their secretive double lives. It's just nothing that any of the agents spoke about, ever. Your kids weren't ever supposed to know. Neither was anybody else outside of "The Community" for that matter. And for good reason, it worked. Screwing up and outing someone could cost you your life or another agents or the life of someone you loved. The first rule of survival in the spook business is guard against leaks, which can be deadly. The shrinks and the legal department would routinely grill case officers working and people attached to clandestine operations like a bull dog lawyer doing a cross-examination. No one could afford to be compromised. A few times the kids had gone "fishing," blown his privacy and trust like a kid looking under the bed for Christmas presents. It was wrong and they knew it and then they went running to Mommy. Fortunately, Mommy was clueless. Hell, Penn had been with the same person more than thirty years and she still didn't know him at all or get it. This amazed him. It confounded him about most women he had known. The kids did what any normal American kid is taught to do–tell a grown up. Sadly, they already were grown up and they should have gone to their Dad first.

But the couple was already at the point where the relationship was nasty and unstable and on it's best day, it was contemptuous. He felt guilty. For so many years he tried to build with her what he grew up with. Penn wanted that crazy familial intimacy. He craved it, prayed for it but it never came. Cold and prone to emotional tirades, she rejected him. She also had none of the same physical needs as Penn. After many years trying to salvage the relationship, it became too draining. Time was flying by and she still didn't know him or really seem to care to. He needed intimacy and warmth and companionship, even if it wasn't real or what he dreamed about. He was ready, willing and able to sacrifice his life and laid it on the line in two areas. After many years though he just couldn't do it in the third arena. So after a while he shut down emotionally and spent more time away working because it was just easier that way.

They couldn't fight if he wasn't there. It wasn't good for the kids and he could not bring himself to leave them. So he stayed. The girls never knew and they grew up thinking that everything was fine. Or at least normal. "When I was at home I missed the work and when I was in the field I missed the girls."

As they got older, he welcomed the chance to have the kind of relationships with them he had wanted his whole life. He could speak to them as people, not as babies anymore. Putting stock and validity in their exchanges, he loved it. It was precious to him. He was amazed how his drive to protect them had not diminished as they became more self–sufficient. He hoped that they never found the stash of weapons and secret things he kept hidden at home and hoped that they never needed to know about Kevlar vests, silencers and amour piercing rounds that weren't standard issue in the regular world. He was used to having to cover his tracks professionally, but he hated the fact that he had to mask his real identity and purpose in his every-day home life. He was really just a goody–goody when push came to shove. For him deception was more of an effort than a skill that came to him naturally. At heart he was a choir boy, it's just that his business could get very ugly and usually involved the highest of stakes.

Thank God he was in the field again…disguised as a high pro-file journalist on the world stage and then at the appointed time, he would zero in on his real mission. He could embrace any loca-tion. Washington, NYC, Paris, Oslo, hell even LA. He never liked LA, especially the people, but anything was better than Pakistan. With the number of Middle Easterners in LA, it could feel like Amman or Abu Dhabi on any given day.

But he was hell and gone from Formula One tracks, good architecture, polo mallets and Hermes bags. He grew up average. An average American kid but now he knew the difference and he was well aware that one side had it all over the other, and there was no doubt about which side had the favor of the gods. It wasn't the current group that was bowing five times a day and hunting his American ass.

CHAPTERSEVEN

The café he was sitting in was playing a very bizarre mix of what could only be described as Middle Eastern, Indian influenced, French techno. The kids seemed to think it was okay, but it was the weirdest shit he had heard in a long time. He would have given his left nut for the familiarity and the calming affect of The Beatles, The Beach Boys, Skynyrd or even Patsy Cline. He wondered what the kid who composed this musical masterpiece parents looked like. Holy hell he thought, where did the two people who gave birth to this kid meet?

He tried to wrap his head around such trivialities and dissect everyone who was caught up in their own activities around him. He wondered if the grape leaves would taste as good as he remembered and whether he would have the time to enjoy them; he had left a trail of destruction on the mission he had just completed. He could feel his stomach screaming at him. He always got testy when he was hungry; it takes a lot of calories to move a big body. Since this was a locals only joint there was a chance that the fare was still his kind of food, substantial and seasoned just enough to delight his taste buds. He avoided neighborhood cafes; the last thing he needed was a gastro-intestinal adventure. All the same it was a constant risk outside of the US; and so he usually carried Company issued antidotes in his pocket. Hell, while on assignment he almost always packed a bottle of Pepto-bismal in his inside jacket pocket and drank it like it was Kool-Aid.

Yea, if he was messed up the only place he would want to be is Israel… amazing doctors there, the next best place to NY or Mayo or LA or Washington. His thoughts bounced around some more about the girl with the gorgeous legs that he couldn't wait to examine up close and personal.

He didn't know that she had many friends and had spent time in the Middle East or that she had grown up in a Catholic family like him. The difference was that her family kept an Israeli flag in the closet next to the Red White and Blue and grasped the delicate balance of power and democracy in the Middle East.

Her Dad had spent a great deal of time in France, Italy and North Africa and had a real handle on geo politics in the region. He started training her as a child. Geography, topographical details, logic, how to care for her body medically and make it formidable. He impressed upon her the importance of listening and observing people in their environments. It never dawned on him that he was building a future operative. Her choices of what to be when she grew up were always different for a girl... pilot, pirate, surgeon, spy. She played army with the boys and enjoyed handing boys their asses, she loved tree forts and hiding in fields with army gear.

One day while visiting the graves of her Dad's parents she told him how afraid she was. He took his daughter aside, and told her straight out. "Don't ever be afraid of dead folks." She asked him why, so he told her. "Baby, they are the only type of person that can never hurt you." It made perfect sense to her in that day in the sunshine. He educated her to so much. He taught her to be self sufficient, and a lone wolf, like him ... He encouraged her to try everything and not to be fearful, and put no stock in anyone else's opinion except her own, based on her own experience. Penn had no clue about any of this that day when he sat in that restaurant, thinking while trying to stay focused on keeping his ass intact, so he could discover once and for all what it felt like to hold this girl in his arms.

He watched the door for the first ripple of the curtain to signal someone's hand on the door. How could he know what the future would bring? He had yet to figure out that he had met his match. But this, like all good things would come in time, like how tiny seeds become trees in which you can build a house. Aria was only interested in being a tree in which he could build a house. She felt that given what he did professionally he deserved no less, in fact she was sure of it.

Months from now, he would come to know curled up next to her in any number of beds around the world, an inner peace and warmth that he had never experienced previously. He would be peaceful and light whenever they were together. It never mattered where they were or what they were doing, only that they were preferably squirreled away in a dimly lit room together. Curtains drawn laying around like big cats on the Serengeti on top of one another proud, protective and open. This would become their time that belonged only to them, not to the good of the world or any organization in it. In a selfless way, they were hunkered down to preserve their sanity and the sanctity of their relationship; during some very hostile times for a couple of goody–goody throwbacks on a mission with a soundtrack.

Little did Penn know while he sat dining alone wary of his surroundings that Aria was on the other side of the world tuned in to what was going on with him. All while she went about her days and nights secretly losing her mind with worry for him. She could tell no one about their predicament. On one occasion that summer while in a store shopping, she had a moment of emotional nudity in front of a complete stranger. Penn called her after returning to the safety of a controlled situation. She was so relieved to hear his voice after an extended blackout period, that the minute the secure sat link connected she ran to the side of the store facing a wall and dropped her purse to dig for a pen to take notes.

The whole time listening and the passion in her whispers her body language alerted a shopper in the nearby greeting card section. She became aware immediately that a middle aged lady was stealing glances at her with love and pity. Aria burst into tears. Not usually the type to tip her hand, she suddenly felt naked in public. But she didn't give a damn. For the first time, she started to wonder what would happen in their future. Still unbeknownst to him she was cabled to him body and soul through the best and worst parts of what he was experiencing in the field. Inhabitants of a visceral and volatile world that would come to be known as their existence. Their physical, intellectual, spiritual and emotional playground…

CHAPTER EIGHT

Over the next year, she was introduced, albeit very slowly, to a series of situations and people in and around "The Company." She introduced him to some people as well. She started relationships with people for him in order to help him at work and to put good guys where they needed to be. The groups had become so cubby holed and specific to keep everyone safe that it was hard to get alphabet soup groups to work together. It was completely a security issue, nothing else. Everyone she dealt with as a friend, family or lover was protected and trusted her completely. Aria always made a point of voicing her true intentions. She would start sentences with "This is my goal or this is what I want and here's why I'm doing what I'm doing." People had the option to engage or not, to meet and befriend someone or not. If they worked together or had coffee or sex outside of their work or whatever that was their choice not hers and she never put pressure on anyone. Aria just had a handle on who would be good together and who would protect each other. She never pulled anyone in that did not have the best of intentions, true patriots only, everyone else need not apply. She cared only about the quality of the character of each person.

As usual Penn was stuck in Pakistan. As much as he loathed being there and wanted to get the hell out, but he was going nowhere until he finished his mission. Everything about it sucked. He loved the work and mission, he just loathed the place and the behaviors of most of the population. At least he had been there enough times that he knew the basic things that got a person with fewer survival skills killed. Like someone who thinks that flying by the seat of their pants in a hell hole like this will work. Islamabad always feels like you're on another planet, surrounded by alien creatures. Everything is assaulting; every minute of everyday. Anyone who says it's a beautiful culture is either stupid or needs to have their head examined. For a westerner who is used to clean water and air, electricity, a safe food supply, indoor plumbing, religious tolerance and respect for the female gender, Pakistan, like Afghanistan, sucks. There is just no way to get comfortable in Pakistan.

Penn knew the minute he hit the ground running that he needed to find water, no easy chore. Fortunately for him he knew some of the local purveyors. He learned to recognize the local labels that were safe and so he stockpiled them the entire time that he was there like a squirrel that stockpiles nuts in multiple hiding places. It wasn't much different when it came to food. He was always scavenging for food. Where could he eat? Where was it safe? Who sat where? Where could he pick up snacks? He had food stockpiled in a safe place and on his person always... the survival stash.

"You never come between a big guy and his safe food supply in the third world, he will take you out without blinking, then he will go back to Kansas and take his kids to see Sesame Street on Ice, hug puppies and make love to some hot blond wife who can drive a truck, plane, stroller and a tractor and it's all in days work for him, no virgins included. Mentally stable and healthy as all get out, eat your heart out, towelie." "You're looking at a happy man that Jesus, Buddha and Jewish folks are all just fine with; everyone but Allah. Boo Frickin Hoo, he felt so bad. Tough shit. He was there to save people, millions of them, the world over." The scumbags that he crossed swords with didn't care who they killed ... Israelis, Americans, Brits, Aussies, Indians, Germans, French, Danes. "Their game was destruction on a massive scale. They just don't give a damn, never have never will. He learned for all the pushing and pulling and years in the field, there was one thing was for sure: you can't change people's DNA, and in Pakistan, it is what it is." Same drill different day.

What's more Penn wasn't about to let all the new found political correctness and diplomatic niceties crowd out common sense based in time tested experience with battling jihadists. He knew what he was there to do, and he would not let fear of retribution from novices compromise his safety or his mission on behalf of the "Free World."

For all the brusque exterior Penn had a soft emotional side. He had met many little boys all over the world with hunger in their bellies that had not been brainwashed, he would have liked to have taken them back to the U.S. and given them a new life, but it wasn't possible and it broke his heart regularly. The other reality was that America had to screen at this level. The U.S. was about the only country in the world that allowed pretty much anyone to immigrate. Unlike most other civilized nations, Uncle Sam didn't charge for citizenship or require a prescribed level of education. The average American was oblivious to such facts. They were certainly not going to learn this from the popular press and no one seemed more in the dark than the younger generations as no one was bothering to teach them civics. Pop culture and the current administration were involved in their version of a game, "We suck, excuse us while we kiss your ass." All the operatives on the ground saw the daily outcomes, the lack of foreign policy experience and the catastrophic worldwide mayhem that antics like that got us into. The "new cluelessness" angered and frightened every single person it touched at home and abroad.

Most of the younger generation bought being lied to, they didn't have any frame of reference, they had never wanted for anything, they were fat and happy. For the most part, it was only the lucky kids with military families who spent time being raised abroad that really knew the score. Most Americans had no grasp of how most of the world really lived and we are not talking about London or Paris.

We were by no means perfect, that was not the point, but we had a much better track record than any other group in history. When we put boots on the ground we always left and the only ground we asked for was the land to bury our dead. There was a reason that an African kid came to the States to get a doctorate. He would drive a cab, start at the bottom leaving his wife and child; only to bring them years later when he could manage a decent apartment and wage. The worst thing you can do to a human being is to steal his dreams, take away his will to achieve and work. People must push and achieve in order to maintain the will to live. Why do you think scientists tell you not to feed the animals? Because it's a moral imperative that the adult animals teach their young to push and hunt. It's about survival... surveying the America he loved, Penn saw too many people with entitlement issues. To him they represented a waste of what could otherwise be productive lives, which he considered the price of admission to the human race.

To be lucky enough to be born into a democratic republic with options and freedoms. Everyone had something to offer, it was a gift plain and simple. In most places Penn got sent, "you never got the option to change your lot, period." He couldn't believe in something for nothing. Everyone he knew had worked way too hard for everything they had, and earned. "Their cost was time away from their families, often written in blood in the service of their country." People who were slackers had no place in their world and Penn often thought about this as he saw people struggling to survive in various parts of the developing world. "Real struggle, not someone trying to payback college loans that they chose to pay back after graduation from Harvard." Whining made him roll his eyes. In NY or Washington where he would often have to meet with some new rocket scientist of a girl, where she would flip her hair and bitch about a broken Lexus taillight and a ticket that she got because she was on her cell phone in Jersey. With so many Americans taking their blessings for granted, Penn and some of the other operatives, the guys and girls on the ground, sometimes questioned themselves about why they put their lives on the line time and time again.

In his case his ability to see the positives had gotten better lately. There was a girl, who was the girl of his dreams, and he had her and dreams of a future to protect. She didn't take anything for granted and put everyone else first. She wasn't typical head down and ass up in twitter. People got her respect because they earned it and she didn't trade on her looks. She worked her ass off 24 / 7. He respected the hell out of her. She was as relentless and unstoppable as any confident man he had ever known anywhere. She would march through fire for the right cause and he knew better than to ever say no to her or dare her to do anything. Penn was a quick study on her personality traits. All the same of it, he wanted to sleep with her and love her but he also thought "The Company" should clone her. He wondered if they were hip to that yet, because if they weren't, he sure as shit wasn't gonna tell them. They had enough ideas already, they didn't need any help from him.

The phone hadn't stopped buzzing since he sat down at the restaurant. All this had happened in a relatively short period of time and so he took a few phone calls. His belly was doing flip flops so he ordered a diet Coke while he waited. One of the calls was the embassy, an attaché informed him of a change in meeting place and he was asked to make a stop very quickly. He sucked down the soda to calm his belly, paid the bill left a tip in the local currency.

As he walked out on to the street he was hit by the stench, the noise, the pollution and the call to prayer. It was oppressive. So he was happy to hide his eyes behind his sunglasses and he used them to obscure his true intentions. He headed for where he had to make contact with a government mole–a risky but often necessary activity in his trade. It was now his job to get to a park between the restaurant and the embassy and then to the embassy by a certain time. But at least there he could eat while he did a meeting and then do some research on some other people he was supposed to meet for dinner. He was supposed to meet some operatives with the Pakistani Intelligence Service and he needed to find out who he could trust. The mole had proven to be a reliable ally on previous forays into this hellhole and Penn was counting on him more than ever now. He had learned previously that the home office while usually armed with the latest intel, sometimes was behind the power curve and he could not afford any miscalculations. Penn jumped onto the packed street and hopped into a little peddle bike pull cart. For short trips on side streets this mode of transportation often worked better than cabs and people didn't look twice at them. He had about twelve blocks to walk to the park and the dilapidated sidewalks were damn near unnavigable. They were packed with people, vendors, carts and animals. It reminded him of a seedy shore boardwalk. It could at times get more than a little strange.

In NYC the funniest thing you might see is a bad drag queen in broad daylight, but in this part of the world you could see almost anything; and it could be gut wrenching; extreme poverty, corpses, women being beaten and stoned, abandoned starving children wandering the streets like stray dogs and cats. Altogether it was a collection of your worst nightmares all realized right there in living color. Welcome to Pakistan. Days before he'd been in London where he had flown in from Washington, high profile just like a tourist on holiday. He came through with the usual stuff. His clothes for the higher end functions and all his garb and shoes for the giant litter box. It was quite a contrast, tuxes and slip–ons, dress shirts together with throw away t-shirts and khaki pants and cargo shorts, boots, gym shoes and Italian sandals. It was like a schizophrenic fashion spread. There was no rhyme or reason to the inners of his luggage unless you knew what he really did for a living. There would be a few articles that would need to be swapped out or ditched once he hit the ground, but at least he would have two days in London to rest, eat and prep. Running thru his head repeatedly like always, the joke…prep, prep, prep, fingers crossed pray, Now we go. Heathrow was always comforting, the last little bit of home before all hell broke loose in whatever form hell happened to take at any given time.

Good ethnic food, people he was comfortable with on our team and theirs, great MI 6 relationships and the last familiar things that he could count on. People that ran pretty much on the same program and had no language barrier. This just gave him one less thing to worry about. Not that there were language issues at this point in his career. He understood and spoke most of the languages needed to take care of business. He was lucky, he was told he had a great ear and an affinity for languages, thank God. He blew through baggage and customs without a tail and down into the area where there was a team to meet him. He recognized his friendlies and walked out to a black bulletproof vehicle. More of our local guys were waiting to see their buddy. The minute he was in the safety of the tinted windows they pulled away from the curb and he was handed a leather duffel bag containing some of the tools of his trade. Inside the case was also a sealed envelope with some of the details of this operation, the latest intel on the situation and a breakdown of his schedule for the next 36 to 48 hours. Now that he was in a safe situation he paused, acknowledged his people in the car and then his mind wandered to one more place, home, the East coast where Aria would be in the middle of her day. He didn't know what she was doing but he couldn't wait to find out. He shot off a quick text to her right there in front of everyone and hoped that she would see it and reply.

For all the wonders of technology, it often failed. Penn hoped that he would get to make a phone call to her and it was all he could think about besides getting back to Washington. When he got to his room he would have to find food and water, get briefed and check in. Penn knew his comrades would want to monopolize his time as much as possible just as they were trying to do in the car while he was taking inventory of the contents of his newest black bag. He would still rather do that alone in his room. Back on the East coast Aria was waiting, pacing and worrying and waiting for him to get into his next semi–controlled situation at least for the time being.

CHAPTER NINE

Today she had been up since the crack of dawn–worrying about him pretending to work, she wanted to make herself busy enough to distract her from the real reason that she could not sleep. Waiting to know that he was down and safe. Their relationship even in the beginning was never "Twitter", it was never done in "real time" because of security concerns; Langley routinely held messages up screening them to protect Company operations and Penn and then later Aria. There were extended time lags and messages got lost in cyberspace. It seemed everyone and everything were constantly changing locations. Langley watched over everything the couple did to preserve life and limb.

Penn and his companions finally arrived at his hotel room. It became a constant spy game of musical chairs, it had to be. Two of his wingmen checked the room out and swept it for listening devices while another operative scouted the lobby and the floor and rest of the building and surrounding area to make sure that there was no trouble lurking. No one knew what was up, but everyone understood about certain agents being specific, expensive and unique, so Penn was treated like a prize polo pony from time to time. This was one of those moments. All the guys on the ground only got a piece of the pie. Need to know basis only. The guys were always around, but never when or where you would expect. They disappeared into their jobs just like Penn. After a few moments, they informed Penn that they would return in about four hours to retrieve him.

Now that he was alone, he quickly opened his newest duffle for the second time and checked it thoroughly making sure he had everything he needed. Satisfied, he checked in with Langley. Confident everyone was holding up their end, he opened his suitcase, pulled out his toiletry kit and ditched his clothes. He felt dirty and wanted to shower before trying to reach Aria. Penn also wanted to try to get some sleep but he wanted to hear her voice and a mental image to be the last thing in his head before he nodded off. He cracked open a bottle of Evian from the table and carried it and his toiletry kit into the bathroom. He fired up the shower, set it to steaming hot and stepped in. He immediately felt human again. Penn fantasized about having her there with him and making love to her in the shower, wondering if she would be up for anything like he was. He hoped so. He stepped out and dried off. He wrapped himself in a towel and slid between the sheets, grabbing his phone on the way into the bed. He wanted to crash for just long enough to be able to string coherent thoughts. He just wanted to have time to speak to her and not be rushed. He got up again to double check the lock on the door and shut off the light. He quickly shot off a text to home base politely telling them "to leave me the fuck alone for a few hours, because I need sleep." He tried to reach the girl but only got her voicemail. He was disappointed. "Shit!" He always took it personally when she missed calls. It was crazy but he did it anyway. He figured he would try again in a hour or so.

He thought about the day they had discussed when he would return to Washington and she would come to see him. That day couldn't arrive fast enough. He was flying. Then he remembered drifting off to sleep with eyelids that felt like they had miniature weights tied to them. He thought about all this while he was in the back of a peddle bike. Shit, he really was in Pakistan and it still sucked. He wished he was back in London like in his daydream, prepping for meetings and dinners with the U.S. Ambassador and other Embassy personnel. But sadly no, he was definitely still in Pakistan and it was no longer the beginning of his trip. It wasn't London, he was nearing the end of this field trip–at least he was almost to his destination.

Penn was nearing the end of three long hard weeks and he could hardly wait. In that period of time he had taken care of business in seven different countries; and he was still alive. "Bonus!" Pakistan was the final leg and soon he would be jetting home, thank God. The peddle bike pulled to a stop. He paid the driver and got off the contraption. He had an uneasy sense that he was under surveillance, so he ducked into a ramshackle of an eatery, proceeded through the building to the kitchen and exited a back door. No one said a word to him; he had that "Don't fuck with me" look about him.

He walked into the park and met his contact and got what he needed from him. Outside doubled back and walked a couple more blocks until he was at the embassy. Penn was buzzed into a secure area and checked in again. He was put in a holding lobby until he was greeted by the military attaché and some other folks at a reception. He made the necessary rounds and then sat down, feigning interest in the goings on; he knew where all the players were already so this just felt masturbatory. Penn knew what he had to do and it wasn't there. He was just doing what he was told and showing his face. In his job it was all about appearances. He sat down at a table where his place card was displayed and had a drink. He slipped into a momentary daydream. He compared this shindig to the embassy parties in London, Mares and Madrid and at all the other places in the world, where he had been dispatched. The similarities, the differences, the people, the food, the skull- duggery of it all. "The other countries and their outposts of whatever sort always intrigued him; some were like McDonald's, like how government buddies could feel like a piece of home just about anywhere."

"Embassy personnel, which is essentially spooks operating under the guise of foreign service staff, when they weren't gathering intel for the home team, they were generally doing their best to fuck things up big time for the bad guys." "Sometimes, the support system when you needed it felt like a blanket from your very own room." "It made you feel like a child and you were always grateful for it." Penn waited for about ten minutes while everything was taken care of before he was ushered in behind closed doors.

The local consulate tart came in to offer "her services" before he was in front of a group of people. She was apparently not intelligent enough to understand that he was already "working" and that "a date" was not his current mo. He thought about it just long enough to try to affix a number to her. Congratulations! you're the lucky 1 millionth customer! Here's your free box of cereal! This girl may have been working in Europe but she was "a type" that Penn and every other guy with half a brain knew well. Penn thought she should have had a tramp stamp on her back that said "next" which was not something that appealed to him at this juncture. He cracked a smile at how much of an ass he was being in his own head. Oh well he thought he had been sitting there reflecting on earlier segments of his trip and he was perturbed that he was so far from Aria. Suzanne, like most of them, was a carnival ride. She was cute and she knew it, she had flirting down to an art form. Suzanne hit on any guy on assignment from the U.S. "Ya seen one ya seen 'em all" thought Penn, "bor-ing."

Lost in his head Penn remembered being in London last week; where he boarded a commercial flight bound for Tele Aviv. He was okay with going to Israel. The drill was much the same there as everything that he had done before and he had been picking up the op tempo. The second he hit the ground in Tele Aviv he was aware of the hourglass. Penn was picked up by a band of friendlies and ferried straight to one of our electronic intelligence gathering installations and stayed there. He went to sleep and then woke to call Aria. Too many time zones in too short a period of time. I'm so affected, he thought to himself, but he was in the best place in the world considering...

The Israelis got it, they understood Americans and how to protect themselves and us. Penn always slept while he was there. Three hours in a crash pad, then fresh intel. Then SSDD, same shit different day. Food, crunch time and head grinding intel. Theirs and ours, some phone calls to the kids back home and a get together with some of the locals for some dinner and drinks. He wanted and needed to do all of it, but all he could think about was the upcoming heavy duty crap and returning to his quarters to get some sleep. He needed to call Aria and have more than a three minute conversation, where he would lie about what he was up to. Tomorrow he would be sitting in briefings all day and it would be imperative that he was firing on all jets. The following day there would be a change of venue and it would be game on. From then on out there would be no day dreaming. He knew what was coming and it would not be pretty. Ahead of him were meetings galore with contacts with people who were either on our side or sympathetic. Some meetings were arranged by our people locally on company payroll and some were set up by coordinators in the Langley office. Even though Penn trusted the relationships that were facilitated on his behalf; he was always on guard and viewed them with suspicion. Information was only given on a need to know basis and he never liked being exposed to more people on the ground than was absolutely necessary.

He had to attend one event and often receptions whether they were in Washington, London, Moscow or Tokyo these exercises always unnerved people in his circle, guys and girls alike. Agents never appeared nervous, since they were trained not to tip their hand. But everyone was secretly emptying their bladders obsessively before arrival at any function like nervous canines.

CHAPTER TEN

Conditioning your body and psyche to lie is one of most difficult things to accomplish. It takes years and Penn was really good at it. He had been around the embassy for about twenty minutes when he laid eyes on a new person that came to the party. It was one of Penn's targets, one of the people he was supposed to meet through an intermediary tomorrow. He couldn't believe the size of this guy's balls. He strutted into the room like a cock in a hen house, robes flowing. He smelled like new money that had no redeeming value and had been stolen or inherited, versus earned. Pompous and condescending, he looked down at all the world's "little people." He was from a big family and could make anyone disappear. Penn couldn't stand such arrogance; he had a visceral reaction. Such self absorbed people ran contrary to everything that he stood for. Penn had remembered and tracked him a few days earlier, after crossing into Yemen with a friendly from Israel. The encounter had been arranged by a go between. Penn "set off in a jalopy into the Sinai desert with a frickin Arab covered in baked on dust who smelled like complete shit, but he was an asset working for U.S. intelligence." Driving to the middle of the proverbial nowhere Penn was never so scared–he had been alerted 24 hours earlier that there might be a greeting party, and it wasn't 27 vestal virgins. He was ordered and prepared to take evasive action and didn't see any need to try to be a hero.

It took more than twenty four hours and that whole night in the desert in some piece of shit ramshackle nomadic hut freezing his balls off, he dared not sleep. It wouldn't be safe to make a fire. That would guarantee a swift capture and a Hefty bag funeral. His biggest fear was getting jumped by a group of local Jihadies and ending up in hefty bag being eaten by birds of prey somewhere near the Yemen border, with everyone watching from home by satellite like it was a bowl game.

He was following a lead that led them to at least two targets, who had a hand in the butchering of a deeply embedded fellow agent. A few raging assholes had escaped justice, and Penn's best case scenario was the bad guys being sanctioned with extreme prejudice. He was so looking forward to being the lead man in that particular wrap-up. The pitch, the swing, and then being the one to park the ball. Mickey Mantle, The Babe, Shaq, Ruth, Jeeter, Jordan pick your sports hero; Penn wanted to be that guy. Back in the states there were loved ones of the assassinated agent who would never know that the agency had been taking care of them at arm's length for years and that this was the moment that the whole agency had been waiting for to even the score in their friends' name. Penn thought that if he and his team were able to take care of business, that would be enough. It made everyone feel better to know that the company always took care of its own and that they were never forgotten.

Penn would let the appropriate people know that this guy had showed his face earlier than expected and therefore forced Penn's hand, giving the agency a twenty-four hour advance. It would now be up to Penn to find a way to terminate this wart on the ass of progress by early morning. He would follow his quarry when he left the party and strike at the most opportune moment. This one was payback for everyone in the agency, and he didn't traverse two additional hell-holes and their bullshit to drop the ball now. This was a picture perfect situation and this guy was toast. Penn had a new spring in his step. He left the table and quickly went to the bathroom to double check his weapon and send a text to Langley about what had transpired. He knew they would be pleased. This wasn't the first time that being in the right place at the right time had paid off. His job always was the poster child for chaos theory. Sliding back into the reception, he quickly asked some "pretty thing" to slow dance and watched the man and his entourage the whole time. While he danced he pretended he was so into the girl that he led around the dance floor. Mayhem and payback on his mind. "I cannot wait to eat this guy's lunch."

The whole time he was practicing, his partner never the wiser. She began to ask personal questions and suggested that they find a more private area. Penn was having no part of it, no matter how eager she seemed. He was busy, watching the scumbag circulate and press the flesh, schmoozing with foreign service professionals and assorted women as he sipped a small cocktail. His henchmen kept a close eye on their terrorist friendly meal ticket. Diplomats, spies and whores, Penn wondered what the difference was between all three types of people. Turning his attention back to his "date," he pretended the whole time that the woman he was dancing with was "The Girl". In actuality, "The Girl" was the only girl he was interested in leading around any dance floor. Having observed for a couple of songs, he needed to ditch his dance partner for her own safety and reposition himself. His target was about to exit the party. He gave the tart some cash for the bartender's tip and asked her to go get them drinks while he went to the men's room. She thought she was going to get lucky with some guy from the embassy, so she obliged him and headed toward the bartender, cash in hand. He slipped out of the ballroom in what looked like a casual slide toward the toilet and the common area outside the banquet room. Then he was gone. He made his way outside the building and tagged the car that the "sheik of the week" wedged his fat ass into. A GPS tracking device had been planted earlier in the sheik's personal limo so Penn and his fellow agents back at Langley had a perfect ringside seat to his every word. Meanwhile, an eye in sky followed the car to a compound just outside the city.

Once he was sure that the car stopped and that it had reached its destination, he returned to his hotel. After a couple of hours of sleep, he loaded his body with weapons and food, including a powerful laser that could do permanent damage. He dressed like a jewel thief. Nestled inside a hollow leather belt were three miniature grenades compliments of Mr. Gadget. Like a ninja, he covered his face. He let the household think it was a normal night and everyone was safe. Penn climbed out his hotel window in the middle of the night and went rooftop to rooftop and jumped into an alley a couple of blocks away. He jacked a car and went out to that house, climbed a wall and slipped inside a window. It was easy and quiet. By daylight, there were a couple of dead bodyguards, a deceased evil son of a bitch with a penchant for torture and some drugged mixed breed dogs with big teeth. Penn rifled the house to make it look like there had been a burglary. He took their wallets and jewelry, copied the hard drive and stole the cell phones for intel for the home office.

When the CID and the ISI finally got there, the case was opened and shut, just like that. The site was so clean, messy but no prints, no witnesses, no anything. Shit, except for three dead bodies, some stolen property and a couple of stoned dogs eating potato chips and kibble nobody could prove anything. It was almost comical. It certainly was poetic justice, and the few local hip CID / ISI guys knew it.

Penn had a penchant for pulling off high risk solo operations–especially if it meant stealing something in broad daylight, with people nearby. The Company was never pleased because it meant higher risk but Penn had mastered this type of spy craft and had the most extreme collection of souvenirs to prove it. Penn felt that this guy wasn't even worth a trophy so it never even crossed his mind to take anything, he was just happy he was no longer sucking air. Except for the jihadists and the local agents on the take, all the good agents were happy he was gone. There were a couple of good guys in the CID / ISI that were decent human beings. They were being paid with our taxpayer dollars anyway. They knew what was up and were secretly jumping up and down that one more parasite had been removed from their inner circle. The few good guys loved their country and were very upset at having to raise their children in such a corrupt and out of control place. At every turn they were doing all they could to bond with the few families who were like- minded, doing anything they could to drive the religious whack jobs the hell out of Pakistan. To them what the authorities discovered at the house amounted to beautiful, swift justice which they secretly backed. Shaking their heads they pretended to be baffled. All the while, they knew whose calling card was left and they rubberstamped it. The American embassy got a call the next morning to inform them about some "unfortunate murders" that occurred the previous night. Of course, they had to keep the proper authorities in the loop. No one in any of the American intelligence agencies knew anything about it.

The ambassador was also notified that there were several bags of potato chips annihilated around the dwelling, along with a couple of very stoned canines on something akin to low dose elephant tranquilizers that came out of India. As a result, the local police were closing the case. With no witnesses and a couple of stoned dogs, the authorities didn't have a lot to go on. Too bad.

Penn was there to find out how far out their web extended. Pakistan, Afghanistan, where else? Who was responsible for all the terrorism? Earlier in the week Penn had been in Turkey, on a one day run and hours later a government installation was bombed, terrorists. It was twenty four hours following his departure. They apparently had bad intel, because they missed, again. Penn was very lucky. He had always been lucky. He knew he was always in their cross hairs when he was in the region. He thought, "Wow, I was just there yesterday and three days before that. In and out like a drive through, they apparently didn't have enough time for the set up."

There were meetings he flew in to attend, meetings where the locals from whatever region and company got to show off; under the guise of "not being their respective governments." All of the players were so proud of all the new "toys" developed to help defend their home teams. They really wanted to gloat more than anything, certain that such a display would leak back to all involved parties, therefore making the world a safer place.

The world is safer when adversaries know that the other side is serious about defending their turf. Deterrence usually is maintained and countries know that no one can take anyone else's shit. That some country can't just bust down someone else's door and take all their toys, land and resources and kill people. "Most countries outside the U.S. have gotten this message so they have stacked their defenses accordingly." "When one of these third world countries acquires a weapon of mass destruction the first thing they do is brag, set a press conference, grant high level interviews and do things to make journalists do cartwheels, they manipulate the worldwide press into a frenzy." "They like to show off the latest Russian jet that they bought, invite a group of journalists to tour a military installations and parade their soldiers and weaponry on the world stage and then expect reputable journalists to write riveting stories about it all and stick a flag in it and call it done." "You do it because you have to, because that is what you are there to get done. And it fosters the relationships that allow you to dispose of some scumbag that truly deserved it." That is the real mission... accomplishing it sometimes requires a speedy exit before people catch on to what really happened, sometimes they're into it, they like it and they realize they have assisted in making their and everyone's world a safer place to be. Sometimes they're pissed... this is when things get dicey, when they feel like they have been duped or used.

CHAPTER ELEVEN

When some asshole gets checkmate, and innocent people suffer it constitutes a loss for everyone. However, if some jihadist makes an unscheduled exit and it saves millions of lives down the line because we or someone else move a chess piece in the correct moral direction, people need to be okay with it. People need to grow up and get real. "Whip out the big kid underoos!" Penn knew and lived it every day. Through airports and cab rides and donkey rides and trekking in the desert. On private planes and trains and helicopter rides, sexy cars, fighter jets, motorcycles, piece of shit cars and trucks and ships of all configurations and every other form of transportation you can imagine. Penn did it all regularly, whatever it took. Penn hit the airport coming back from the day trip to Istanbul. Everything had been going well. He had just over one day left and was anxious to get finished with his last few charges in Pakistan and get the hell out. It could not happen soon enough as far as he was concerned. Tomorrow was the best case scenario or the next day at the latest. Penn got an escort from the airport back to his hotel and munched on the snacks in his briefcase while sitting in the back of the car. He was just eating in advance habitually, nervously.

For once he didn't even care about food. He just wanted to get back to the hotel and call the home office and describe to them what had happened earlier in his day. He also needed to transmit information back to the home office and he was wondering when this would be possible. He needed to call Aria and lie to her, not telling her that he had been somewhere else for the day. He wondered what she would think about his insane running around, his crazy life, and what it would be like to have what everyone else pretty much considered a normal day. He wondered too whether she had normal days, like he thought she did. It had been so long since Penn had one and it dawned on him, that he really didn't know how to define it. But he had to admit that just the concept alone was quite alluring. The sexiness of normalcy or of what he could remember that it was. To be able to wake up and know where you were, not to struggle to remember what country you were in, to not have to sleep with a weapon, to know that your dog had to be walked, all of the little things that people tend to take for granted. The trappings of normalcy, the voice of a day. What Penn did not know yet was that Aria was not what most people would consider normal, not by a long shot. And it was a good thing because what Penn wanted had nothing to do with normal anyway; he only thought it did. In fact as defined by most people, it had absolutely no place in either one of their worlds.

Foolishly, most people only think they would sign on for a wildly exciting career in espionage around the globe, but most people are seriously risk averse and run from discomfort, it's self preservation and human nature. Penn and Aria's work and relationships required that they run towards danger, that they repel down the precipice, that they walk the line without a net nearly everyday. There were two little rules that both had been taught separately and both lived by, but never discussed as time went on because it was understood and they didn't have to. Don't look down and don't get caught. Very simple words to live by that made all the difference in the world.

Back at the hotel after the side trip and another shitty Pakistani cab ride from the airport Penn could breathe at least for a spell, he thought. For all his rough inner dialogue and his current environment, he was genteel. Penn was raised in the South by parents who were a first generation European immigrant and a gentle Southern lady and her mother. He was a gentleman, so his speech, mannerisms, education and intelligence reflected such; but he could respond like any number of his fellow operatives when the shit hit the fan in the field and he did not mince words, clearly he was no candy ass. He was a formidable intellect with a velvet gloved gentlemen's hand. This never went to waste back at the home office where he was often used as the ultimate spokesman. This happened more regularly now and he had finally become okay with his charge. After years in the game he was supremely confident and knew his capabilities. Still, he had to focus a bit longer and then he could finally leave.

Penn felt he could handle almost any situation, except navigate with this girl. He felt quite literally that he had just lived his life up to now waiting for her to be born and grow into something he could wrap his head and body around. It was all he wanted, to go home, safely and to get to her as quickly as possible.

Ahead of him was one more meeting maybe two in a hotel, this afternoon. Everyone at home base was tuned in and knew it had been set. So much of his job was just that, hurry up and wait. It's usually in God awful places on the planet. Waiting… "Waiting for other people to get their shit together and then all of a sudden, bang all hell breaks loose, and you better keep your eye on the ball, or you could wind up dead." Penn got a call from the home office and another from his chief operations coordinator, Marshal Tedowski, who was blowing off a steady stream of new intel information in his ear. Marshal, who was the personification of a loveable shit storm, was intolerant of anyone who didn't have the intellectual capacity or the emotional tenacity to keep up with him.

Marshal, who had known Penn for more than 20 years thought of each other as brothers and used to call each other such when no one else was around. Like so many of the guys Marshal was the physical antithesis of Penn. He was round, and was a poster child for lousy eating habits, lack of sleep and was frenetic in absolutely everything in which he participated. In Washington, a city that pretends it's still a genteel Southern town Marshal was a social pariah although he never thought of himself that way. Washington is a town of professional liars, bullshit artists, international thieves, and whores, it's no place for an honest man or woman or their children. When one shows up at the arrival gate at Reagan or Dulles, alarms go off all over Capital Hill and Pennsylvania Avenue. An honest hard working person who also has power and position and is fearless makes everyone look bad. The prevailing attitude is that the person must be crushed quickly instead of understood. He or she is the proverbial square peg in a round hole. That was Marshal. The issue with Marshal is that he always ran contrary to the program, he was never a prick. Many people with his job description to a certain degree serve the purpose better if they have the ability to be a son of a bitch. Marshal could play that role, but only because he loved his country.

He simply expected people to do what they said they were going to do. Oh, and here's the kicker, when they didn't, he would call them on it. This was always great at cocktail parties and nothing short of earth shattering around the conference tables that don't really exist in Washington. Marshal and Penn were like Jimmy Stewart in "Mr. Smith goes to Washington" and it wasn't an act. That irritated people on the inside that actually were jackasses. They knew they would never be as good or as smart or as successful. Marshal and Penn were highly effective with their hearts in it for the right reason. They never wrapped themselves in the flag as a political ploy as was the current fashion; they wrapped themselves in the flag for protection and love and because they believed in the people and the documents that built it.

Penn dialed on his com device, Marshal was immediately on the line. "What are you doing Penn?" " "What are you doing "Mom," asked Penn. "What the hell are you Twitter Langley?" "I just got back in the room and everything's fine. Pakistan is still a shithole, no changes to report. Sorry to be the bearer of bad news." "How did everything go in Istanbul? What presents do you have for me?" "I have things from the other night here with our friend who forced my hand, and then I have more from today as well. All the puzzle pieces fit."

"Good, for that you get a gold star and an atta boy. You're having a good day." "How the hell am I going to get this stuff to you sooner rather than later? I'm feeling anxious. I don't want to sit on it any longer than I have to. I'm running out of places to hide shit. This place is a buffet of intel. All you can eat, and I'm done." "Nah, make it work, you're outta there within twenty–four. Hold on to it and transmit the rest. Just fly low with the hand carry, okay?" "Get it worked out." "Yeah, fine, I'll get rid of almost everything after, just confirm transmission for me. I don't need to sweat that too."

"How long before that series of meetings today?"

"Three hours. Shouldn't take very long. The first two should go quick. Really basic stuff. Same place. The third is the change up. The guy that was fixed by the sheperd. Change of venue, sandy pasture, which way is the beach?"

"Only you would get in so deep within a few days that we are actually dealing with a fucking sheperd. Remind me to make a tasteless joke about this later, something to do with wellies. Affectionately known as sheep fuckers."

"No problem, I won't let you forget. But I know this is one you guys will never let me live down. With my luck he is an informant who also is a frickin sheperd, only in the Middle East."

"Just remember, what happens in Pakistan stays in Pakistan, call me after." "Wouldn't miss it for the world, my friend. I'll check in after each meeting, and then after the last one I'll call to make sure that we are still on target for my departure." "Just watch your ass. Don't assume that these guys are as benign and unprepared as they have been in the past. You can never tell how fast or slow they are going to get with the program. Don't take any unnecessary chances." "Roger that, we'll talk in a few hours Chief. Keep any eye on me, I'm a steak guy, not a lamb guy. I don't feel like having any of my last meals be anything but surf and turf.

Remember that. Get me the flock outta here."

"You're funny."

"Yeah, it's one of my hidden and more endearing qualities. Don't tell anyone."

Talk to you later. Roger that, I'm out."

Alone in his hotel room, Penn proceeded to put things in order as he would need them laying them all over the bed. Notebooks, his laptop computer, pens, files to review before each meeting. He so hated being un prepared that he routinely over prepared and sweat it terribly when he did not have proper time to prep. He laid out his clothes for the three interviews. He would be playing the part of the inquisitive journalist. For this gig, however, he would be wearing his token garb to complete the picture for them. Turns out that this would be a good thing anyway, because part of his journalist uniform gear even though it was summer, was Kevlar.

Though it's light and thin for what it is, it's still a bullet proof vest and it's bulky and hard to disguise. It was always a challenge to keep it under wraps. The vest was hot and a total pain in the ass to wear but Penn was happy to have the option. He was seasoned enough to know that he should use it all the time when he was in "The Sandbox."

Days enumerated with meetings like today were always a crap-shoot so it was better to err on the side of caution. He certainly did not tell her that it was busy today and that he was digging in for in the last twenty four hours and talking to some really creepy guys to get some more intel before leaving the country. He never said a word. He talked about the weather, or sex or what she was doing. Never ever about his movements or what he was responsible for or thinking about doing. Penn never told her where or when he was going. After a while, he figured out that she knew that he was basically full of it. For his job, he had to be. When he figured out that she had already surmised all this, he stopped. He just stopped bullshitting her, just like that. From somewhere in Europe, during a trip later in the year he made the jump. He just didn't say any-thing. She would just respectfully ask him questions, and he would answer what he could, and what he couldn't he figured she already knew the answers to anyway, so why bother.

Aria woke up sick this day and couldn't sleep at all the night before. Thinking about Penn and waiting for him to call all night long, the past two days had been nothing short of excruciating. She was hanging over the toilet, begging the powers that be to make her vomit. She was cabled to the bathroom as if Mexico had been a recent vacation stop. Her stomach was completely out of whack. She was having frightening, violent nightmares. She was pale white and looked like a vampire. All the blood drained from her face and she was gaunt. Her mother saw her and was worried and suggested that maybe she should see a doctor. Aria got upset and said she was fine. Aria knew what was happening to her was based entirely on Penn, the man whom she had just met and with that her body was flying red flags. She was worried for him, because she understood in advance exactly what was going to happen to him and his very survival was going to be on the line. This was not an acceptable situation from any point of view. Aria was debating when and how to tell Penn, and if she should even say anything at all. If she did everyone would hear her. The home office was always on the line, then everyone would know. They would think she was a spy and not a patriot. She would scare the shit out of everyone, especially Penn. Since it was his ass that was actually the one in the field. Aria felt it was important that he did not get freaked out any more than he already was. What was she supposed to do? Say, "Hi, I really like you and I know you don't really know me yet but, I'm in love with you and you're my soul mate."

"I know everyone is listening but you're in mortal danger and I can tell you exactly what's going to happen to you. I'm trying to save your life. Don't ask me how I know this and by the way, it's going to get really get bad there so please pay attention because I want you to come home to me." Yea, that would go over real well. Penn was pretty wigged out with what was going on already. Aria knew it was going to get a whole lot harder in fact. He was going to get very uncomfortable with Aria's abilities. It would take him and the agency many months to wrap their collective head around that part of their relationship and fully digest it. Eventually she knew it would be okay–he would get with the program and she wouldn't frighten them so much any more. What no one knew is that she already had predicted many things their first year. Not just big things like political issues and outcomes, but crazy things like high profile murders and pregnancies, health issues and all sorts of things all over the world. It was a very frightening thing to always be way to be ahead of the curve. Aria was taught to hide her abilities for safety since she was a child. Her mother hid Aria because she knew the outcome of being found out would not be positive. From the time that Aria was a child, she was "just tuned in to the world", as her mother used to say. To people, and to everything around them, as a child she developed a habit of asking a lot of questions–but for Aria it was an exercise quite different than it was for most people; she asked questions only to check people's opinions about her answers.

Two months earlier Aria had been standing in line at a posh hotel waiting to check in and she received a phone call while speaking to her lawyer that confirmed her prediction of six months earlier. Her former business partner called Aria, in a panic. There had just been a murder and Aria had told him months before in great detail that it would happen and there would be a violent shooting and more. He never believed Aria and berated her about the warning. He and his wife poo–pooed it so when it actually happened they freaked out and called Aria immediately. The only other witness to Aria shooting her mouth off about it months before and to the phone call was her lawyer. The lawyer who had introduced her to Penn during their first meeting earlier that day. Penn was home from his office by the time Aria and her lawyer were gearing up for their next meeting and Penn was distressed because the lawyer had whisked Aria away. Penn didn't know when or how he was going to see her again.

Aria never made predictions in front of anyone and the one time she did the former business partner and his wife and the hotshot lawyer were the only witnesses. So when they received the phone call about the murder the lawyer flipped out when he realized what had just happened. Aria became the bearded girl at the freaky side show so the lawyer immediately went around the hotel telling her business associates and several high level hotel officers what happened before the dinner meeting.

Aria wanted to be sick she was embarrassed, but everyone just thought the lawyer was drinking. No one was privy to the whole situation months before or the warnings she issued to specific people, but the lawyer was. If Penn had known all of this, he would have been stupefied. If he found out she was a freak that could read the worlds collective mind and his to boot... he would have raced for the exits. Penn was used to a whole different type of danger. Physical danger he knew what to do with, in fact, he was good at it. But emotional danger was a whole different ball game. "Talk about letting your balls swing, it wasn't gonna be pretty."

Aria was different, not like what most people would have thought. Someone who everyone said looks like a classic Hollywood movie star and could stand in front of a room full of lawyers and businessmen. What Penn didn't know was that he and Aria were very much alike and just like him, she could do it all. She only pretended she couldn't because the world can't handle it from a good looking straight young female that looked like her. Not without using "bitch" as the catch all and she was no bitch. She tried to figure out what about being competent, hardworking and giving a damn made her a so–called bitch. She had met many women who really could be described as such and she knew she was nothing like those girls, selfish, insecure, and egocentric. She always made a choice to be kind. One of her favorite quotes was "Kindness should never be mistaken for weakness."

She always thought her qualities made her different and desirable. But mostly it just made her vilified by both men and women. If she had been taught to need people more, it would have made her lonely. But in Aria's case, it just made her strong and self reliant. Aria was a very emotional creature, intensely passionate, but she never spent herself on matters which she deemed unimportant or unworthy. She deemed Penn completely worthy from their very first encounter and she saw few people as worthy. She understood Penn the minute she laid eyes on him and there was no going back. It was not even about sex, it was all about character, intelligence, kindness and capacity to love.

Aria wanted Penn to call her's and no one else's, to make a life and babies with, from the very first instant. She never felt safe and she felt safe with him. Penn had told Aria many times "How he played that first meeting over and over in his head as if on a loop tape." He thought it was one of his most precious memories of them together and how it had gotten him through many days and nights in the field in all sorts of hellish conditions. He would reflect on what he had to live for and why he was alive in this age in the first place. "He felt he was alive to finally meet and be with her."

Penn had finally finished pulling his gear together for his case and it was time to put his clothing in order to complete the illusion for the day of the dedicated journalist. With his Kevlar vest an olive green v neck t- shirt to reduce chaffing and wick his sweat away and because it would help spray should he happen to get shot. Then another white neck high t–shirt, and then his collared work shirt and jacket. The whole ensemble was big enough that no one would know what he had on underneath. He took his trinkets that he used for luck and put them in the pockets of his khakis. He stuffed some food and water in his brief case. He needed regular sustenance so it paid to be self sufficient, especially in the third world. Last but not least, he laid out his weapons, pulling them out of the hidden false bottom in the case that he was carrying. He had to hustle, it was getting late. He had spent close to an hour testing weapons and organizing his gear, putting on his "game face" and running the operational stratagem in his head one last time. Penn had changed his service weapon before this rotation of the operation. He had been anxious about it until a couple days earlier, when he got the chance to test it. He had been in the field in Europe a month before and he had experienced a problem, his weapon jammed and the timing really sucked. He looked to the logistics and support team at Langley to make sure that he never ended up in a position like that ever again. So now he was armed with a new service weapon, and a 9 mm backup piece. Penn had other options of course, since intel operatives facing would be assassins never like to be caught with their pants down, so to speak.

But sometimes it's unavoidable, and then having great hands and feet and a fast head will be the thing that stands between you and St. Peter. He thanked God every day for giving him raw power in that arena and the ability to bring all of it to bear against his enemies regularly. He was lucky that he had hit the genetic jackpot; he never took it for granted. The fact of the matter is he always thought of himself as a modern day gladiator. He felt comfortable in the role his whole life, by now he didn't remember being anything different. His role as a globe trotting journalist was just an act. That was the part he never felt comfortable in. In actual fact, he knew that his discomfort playing that part probably made him more effective and convincing in the field because it gave him access to people and places that otherwise would have set off alarms. With his reluctance to display attention getting machismo, he was better able to blend in foreign capitals, especially in the Middle East. He had nothing to prove, he was the alpha male in every room, unless God decided to pop by. He spent his time trying to confuse the bad guys so he knew better than to beat his chest and just eat their heads; that would have been just a little too "Captain Obvious." All of that would have garnered Penn substantially less intel to turn in. It would all be wasted on those guys anyway...most of them were mouth breathers. They thought that they had much more intellectual capacity than they actually did and most possessed artificially inflated egos at a level that was seriously comical. To Penn their stupidity was like red meat to a ravenous pit bull. He enjoyed choking their chain and toying with them. Whether it was at a chessboard or matching wits.

The oil money that even mid level sheiks and their henchmen controlled in the Middle East was formidable. There was no shortage of people waiting around to tell these men how fabulous they were and meet their every need, stroke their egos, or whatever other body parts needed attention. Which was laughable because being concerned with women and their needs or wants had never been tenants of their culture.

One last check of his on person weapons and he closed his multi-pocketed leather bound case. He zipped it closed and grabbed his key and moved towards the door. It was game on. Passing through the lobby he tried to look unlike the poster child for super heroes who had not spent decades turning his six pack into a twelve pack. Penn hopped into a cab and headed towards the first of two hotels, the agreed on venue for the first two meetings. The place was about ten minutes away, but in Karachi traffic with it's non existent infrastructure and endless sea of humanity and bullshit, this exercise could take an hour. He needed to be on time like a regular westerner because this is what they would expect, but he shouldn't be early. That would be a grievous error. Not helping the bad guys to make things easy was always key. Don't make it easy, make it hard. That was his mantra. The trip over to this particular hotel always fascinated him from the airport to the shiny dilapidated buses of silver, the shabbiness of everything, the extreme poverty, he could never get past it. It was the sight of the impoverished, unattended children that wounded him the most.

It sure didn't look like Orlando or Vegas or any other city in the States, where an entire prosperous way of life had grown up around one singular act of business. He lamented how amazing that obviously in this part of the world that the ruling class had never been one to share it's wealth amongst it's citizens. Strange, because the amount of oil money that flowed was immense. Here it was all about greed and collusion among hypocritical religious zealots. As Penn stared out the side window of the car transporting him, he imagined the whole other–worldly spectacle as a colony of filthy cock roaches, only in place of the roaches there were people. Except the reality of the situation was worse, the top echelon kept everything and starved the rest. If you tried to move within your social group, you were systematically slaughtered. The contrast with the west was staggering and it continually blew his mind.

The cab stopped in front of the first hotel. The first of the day, more to follow, and then tomorrow would be here and he could go back to the airport and get the hell out. He entered the lobby and looked around then he headed for the restaurant. They were waiting for him and after some brief introductions he interviewed his "sources" for the magazine article that they believed that he was developing.

All went well and no suspicions were aroused. Both meetings went off with out a hitch. After a while Penn packed up his gear and made his way out of the hotel. It was getting late in the day and he needed to change locations. He hopped into cab number two for the day and took the short trip across town. Penn shot Marshal a text message on the way to let him know what was up and that he was on track for the day. The cab stopped in front of Penn's destination and out he popped. Upon entering the lobby he assessed the situation. No signs of trouble and it was as comfortable as anyone could be in an operational situation in Pakistan. Meanwhile, back in the U. S., Aria was standing in the kitchen with her mother when she suddenly breathed in deep, turned white and grabbed for the sink so she didn't fall over or pass out. At that same moment half a world away in Karachi, Penn did the same drill again–he slipped into a bathroom to empty his bladder before anyone became aware of his presence. Then he headed up to a room that was reserved for a conference situation. He arrived at the room without incident on time and greeted everyone. There was nothing remarkable about it. Before you could say Karachi sucks, all of a sudden the energy in the room shifted. A bearded Arabic speaking waiter of Middle Eastern origin showed up with a towel on his arm under the guise of bringing them something to drink. He approached Penn and at point blank range shot him in the chest. In an instant, Penn's brain revisited the explosive sound of the gun discharging.

Time stood still, and the room quickly cleared...

In that nanosecond, three things flashed through his mind, an intense longing for Aria, how proud he was of his two daughters, and how the force of the large caliber bullets knocked him onto his back. Penn's mind was fully engaged in the moment, which seemed like it took a hundred years. "You realize that you're gonna get shot, and then you're pissed off." "Then you actually get shot and you know things are immensely fucked up. If by then you're not dead, you try to figure out if you're dying or going to die ... " "Once you establish these watermarks, you react accordingly."

Penn had spent his entire career preparing for this moment. He was alone in fucking Karachi. It couldn't be a hell of a lot worse, unless he had been targeted for torture followed by a televised beheading in some dank Al Qaeda stronghold. His enemies came after him; the hit was that specific. Little did they realize they were in real trouble now, he was alive he wanted retribution and he wouldn't stop until he got it. Laying on the floor, it dawned on him that he had just survived a point blank shot to the chest and "somehow by the grace of God and Kevlar" he was alive. He hurt like hell, he was out of it... he had bruised ribs and the wind was knocked out of him.. His head was spinning, but fuck... he was alive, although his would be assassin thought he was dead. Really dead–Elvis dead. Penn thought, "Exterminating this asshole is going to be perversely, pleasurable." After a few minutes Penn exploded from the floor.

He hauled his huge body up off the floor and made a hasty getaway in the most serious act of self preservation he had ever faced. He had to summon the cavalry to come get him the fuck out of Pakistan. If one executioner knew who he was, there were others who did as well, his cover was blown. Out on to the street and down a back alley...where the fuck was the car? He yelled at Marshall in hushed tones. He needed out immediately! Never fucking mind whatever else is on the agenda, they were just shooting at me, I am so blown. Fuck, Fuck, Fuck, he thought.

It seemed like hours before the team showed up. Finally Penn managed to get back to the hotel, assisted by two heavily armed body guards. He dumped his gear on the bed, wiggled himself out of his kevlar vest and clothes and climbed into a hot shower with friendlies posted nearby. There could be no screw ups from this point or he really would be toast. It would be a matter of distracting himself in the hotel room this night so he could get the hell out before the crack of dawn. It was the longest night ever. The plan was to spirit him out of the hotel. Until then, there wouldn't be whole lot of sleeping going on. Penn's biggest fear was that another jihadist might find out his location; there would be no getting away again and everyone knew it. His teammates were ready and so was he. Until then he was trapped like a rat in a shitty little hotel room in Pakistan. Penn dispatched two text messages to the love of his life and listened to Aria's voice on phone messages he had saved. He pulled a photo of her from and inside pocket of a brief and stared as though she would materialize in front of him. The night could not have seemed longer.

He tried to eat, and spent the bulk of the time on the phone swearing in real time with Marshal "what had gone wrong?" "Fuck, Fuck, Fuck" he thought again.

"I did everything right... where was the goddamn leak?" He tortured himself with all the questions wondering where he could have done something differently, if he could of. "Where was the mistake?" He decided against taking any kind of pain killers for his ribs. He called Aria. He spoke with her under the most dire conditions for the very first time. He lied to her and told her he was fine, just a little on edge "tough day" he said. She sensed his predicament and asked specifically about his dinner for the night. She knew that he was deep in the throws of lying his ass off to her in the name of operational security. He was breaching protocol by calling her in the first place but because he had just taken a point blank hit and didn't know if he would survive the night, he figured that bending the rules a bit and calling her to calm himself down was no big deal. He told her that he couldn't wait to leave, that he was finished there and quite satisfied with everything he had completed. He felt like he had done his job, and that he had been quite successful. He said he was tired and he was ready to come home. He was excited about meeting her in Washington. Penn thought he was being so slick bullshitting her and he had yet to realize that during this one conversation that Aria was consciously making the effort to calm him down, make him laugh even though he felt like a long tailed cat in room full of rocking chairs.

Throughout their entire conversation Penn had been alternating between pacing and packing and obsessively repacking. Aria was hyper ventilating on the other end of the phone, just like him. She knew he was trapped in that room with a very evil world outside and she was praying for the safety and skill of those charged with watching over him until he was on that plane headed home. She spoke to him with such sure footed fervor, so clear headed. She knew he needed her and she never let on, not once. She was flattered that it was she who he chose to call when he was at his most vulnerable, not a family member. A girl that he would die to make a family with. They spoke for as long as it was safe to do so and they hated when they had to hang up because of security. They were both watching the clock. Aria stayed awake all night until she knew he was safely in the air then she slept like a newborn. Penn was finally where he needed to be, safe up in the clouds.

Enroute home Penn slept a little, but only because there had been no sleep the night before and he was exhausted. Marshal was on the flight line driving out to the tarmac to greet him. Marshal's big round shiny face was a sight for Penn's sore eyes and his sore ribs. When Marshal went to bear hug Penn, he winced. Marshal was the only handler in history that could get away with a bear hug on the tarmac. No one dared give Marshal any lip–because his knowledge of anything he wanted to tackle was that formidable.

They sped into Washington in a government vehicle and met people for a short debrief and then Penn was escorted to a safe place. The love and respect between the two men was obvious and Marshal's best friend was not only alive and upright, but he was a hero too. This was the kind of real life story that goes on in the agency forever in their own internal version of a history book. A legend was born, to start to right a wrong and two best friends did it together, and it did not get any better than that.

CHAPTER TWELVE

Penn eventually returned to his daily routine, after his stay down in Washington, which was liberating but ultimately exhausting. He had a very difficult time getting his head together after time out in the field. Penn's most difficult time was making his "Day Job" worth doing. He hated feeling like he was having no impact. The worst thing you can do to a super hero is marginalize them. Think about Superman, krytonpnite makes him weak and more than anything sad. He doesn't know what to do when he isn't saving the world, he loses his place, his sense of purpose. It was actually a real problem, post operational disjointedness. It's not just a readjustment problem or life as an adrenaline junkie, it's a matter of being exhausted and listless.

People have issues finding their point of focus post–op. Part of it is being tired in a primal way most people cannot begin to understand. The shrinks at Langley knew all too well what Penn was experiencing, many of the operatives got it. The feelings of guilt when returning to a place of prosperity and peace were very real, and required considerable adjustment. That was Penn; "lights on" and no one home. To add insult to his angst he missed Aria terribly and he could not wait to see her. Since he returned he had been speaking to her at least five times a day. Speaking to Aria calmed him down and made him feel normal and loved, all the things that he had not felt in a very long time. He had love as Daddy, but not as a man. The women he slept with were mostly cold and calculating so very NYC. He slept with many Asians and there was nothing warm or fussy there, no deep warmth, ever. It was just to meet an immediate need, you got your rocks off–it was biology. Nonetheless it wasn't anything that satisfied him any longer. When he met Aria, it rocked his world. "She was like a Latina without the attitude and the drama." She was so warm, she took care of him and anyone else who needed it. She was generous with her heart, kind to people, children and animals even when no one was looking. It was a testament to her character and how confident she was in herself. He noticed time and time again how she put herself out for people. He was proud of that quality, but he was also very possessive of his time with her from the first day that he met her. He wanted to go to lunch on his own with her and be left alone. In his office on the first day, he could have spent all day right there with her. No one else need apply. As the weeks went on and they made multiple dates and plans to get together, first in Washington and then in Miami. He finally admitted to himself that he was falling for this girl, even though he didn't want to. Penn felt that he wasn't ready, all the same, he was insanely curious and he rushed head first into a journey of discovery come what may. He remembered being in denial only weeks before on July fourth when he was at a beach bonfire and some chick parked herself on a blanket next to him virtually throwing her legs in the air. He had just unknowingly out grown whores of any kind and it was right before a field trip. In the past he would have been all over it, effortless was always a goal, but no more.

He was speaking to Aria on the phone at the time and all he could think about was having her there with him, deep kissing her in the sand in the dark lit by the huge bonfire with fireworks in the sky. What a drag, he thought, having to cope with this attention starved woman who kept trying to get him off the phone with the one girl that he had waited for his whole life. The girl that he wanted and needed; his Beach Boys ballad in the flesh, even though she wasn't born when the song came out. Oh well … nobody's perfect. Penn thought this justified how he felt about everything.

The woman bugging him was a pain in the ass. He wanted her to leave him the hell alone and she just would not let up. He finally had to be a blunt and he felt okay about it. She finally got the message and wandered off. He thought she would never leave. Finally, what a relief he thought. He had enough to think about. He didn't need women, he needed Aria. Little did he know that Aria needed him just as much, and would have done anything in the world to be near him. But they would have to wait. There would be a couple of weeks of prep and then another field trip before they could make it official, and really do that tete e tete in Washington. The phone calls at all times of the day and night continued.

Penn charged Aria with finding the place to stay and she found a cozy boutique hotel that she would stay at in DC for the first time. Aria found a brand new boutique hotel that almost no one knew about. It was a secret hideaway. Aria was a hider and favored little out of the way places, high end and hip, but understated and low on the radar, the polar opposite of Penn. Penn would stay in a corporate hotel. Meanwhile, Aria would find the guy who owned a castle and get him to rent her a wing with only one key, hers. She loved her privacy and was much more private than Penn. Aria usually traveled alone for business and this presented some interesting challenges which are different than those faced by a man. So she learned to be flexible and to hide wherever she went; hunkered down alone in hotel rooms all over the world for safety, peace of mind and so she could control who had access to her time and who didn't. Running around a hotel room and doing her toes before going to a meeting was more her style. Her musical tastes were schizophrenic, like her taste in men and clothes. Aria liked everything to be one of a kind, like her. Different and risky, she was the ultimate girl next door, but only if the girl next door looked like she spent her entire life in Vogue Magazine. She was so unlike anyone that Penn ever dated before, that it was almost comical.

Aria was always a true patriot from the time that she was little and always had a strong sense of self. Her mother would say you could always tell in photographs of her as a young child that she was comfortable in the world and in her own skin. Aria had an unbreakable moral compass and held herself and others to high standards. This was another set of traits that she and Penn had in common. The formative years were very telling for Aria. In her first school play, she was cast as Thomas Jefferson's wife. She was irate that they would not let her play Jefferson. She complained bitterly to her parents about what a unfair situation it was, so she took the part of his wife. She figured out that if she couldn't be the guy who was responsible for everyone, she would then be the girl that had the ability to affect him. That was in third grade, she already had an opinion and an attitude. Aria's favorite dress as a second grader was black.

If Amelia Earhart, GI Jane and Lara Croft had a love child it would have been Aria. There was never any middle ground with Aria; it was all or nothing. It was a quality that Penn adored in her, he loved the fact that she never phoned anything in, he loved her passion for life. "I never would have fallen in love with you if you would have been wishy-washy about anything, including me." The world was full of those noncommittal, apathetic, uniformed, ill educated, people. Penn saw nothing positive in it, neither did Aria.

The dog days of summer finally came to Washington where it's so humid and awful, that it feels like you're breathing through cheesecloth. It went from cold to hot as hell, to humid and hot as hell. Not like Baghdad or Kabul hot, but hot none the less. Aria didn't mind, she was used to it. But Penn on the other hand was immensely bothered by the heat, even though he had lived there for years.

The day finally arrived where they would meet in Washington as they had arranged. He would come into town to pick her up at the airport and they would spend the next few days together. She had booked her room in the hotel she had told him about. It's background, she thought was strange with it's colorful history. She called him and told him in advance in case there was a problem. He didn't think so, but thanked her for being so attentive and her good taste. And so it went, Aria boarded a flight at the crack of dawn leaving the beach and the heat heading north. She blasted into the sky in the little aluminum tube that would deposit her into the lap and the arms of an emotional free fall. Penn arrived at the airport more than an hour early, over prepared and antsy as hell. No one knew how it was going to go down. What would they say when they initially saw each other again, it would be the first time since they first met months ago. So much had transpired since then. He thought about it and so did she as she flew toward their rendezvous. What if they did not get along? What if he didn't like her? What if he didn't think she was smart, kind, for real, or beautiful? What if she didn't like him as much as she thought she would? What if they clashed and the heat over the phone wasn't in the room? After all they still had to work together! What if it was a disaster?

They were a mess in separate places, worried about all the same things. He in his collectable car speeding down the beltway and then through DC singing his Beach Boys songs aloud. How would she look? Would she like his cologne? Would she let him touch her? He was so jacked up to hold her, at least he thought he was and he wondered how far would she let him go? Why was he so flustered, he had never felt like this before. Questioning his game, he barely recognized himself. It had been many years since he had worried about a girl...any girl. What made Aria different? What made her so special? Why was he so bent? Jesus! Aria sat on the plane tying her stomach in knots, drinking soda and feeling guilty for doing so. What if he expected to sleep with me? I don't think I could go through with that much intimacy so soon. What if I don't like the way he smells, if his arms don't feel right? If he doesn't make me feel safe and he makes me feel vulnerable? What if he is still seeing half the female population? Holy crap! Aria wondered what had she gotten herself into? Shit. This was a nightmare waiting to happen. He's going to want to jump me, and I'm not ready. The jet touched down and Aria plugged into her MP3 player to let the music give her some much needed courage.

Sleeping well or at all were rare so, Aria was tired. She plugged in her brain as she thanked the pilot and crew as she disembarked from the 737. She took a deep breath when she got to the top of the gangway. She hadn't been in Washington in years and she was so loaded emotionally that she thought that she would explode. She vibrated from the energy of all the surrounding spooks in close proximity that were crawling Reagan National airport. As a rule nothing scared her, but she felt like she was walking a tight rope blind folded over a windy gorge. She stopped in at the bathroom to urinate and check her face and hair one last time. Then she adjusted her attitude in front of the mirror and grabbed her gear and pushed herself into the throngs of people flowing out towards the meeting area at Ronald Reagan International Airport.

Suddenly she saw him, Penn's eyes met Aria's and he was in one piece. It was magic, nothing short of fireworks at Disney World. She melted all over the floor and she wasn't even near him yet. They locked on each other's gaze and that was that. Her stomach did a flip flop. She let out a squeal and ran to his arms. He wrapped himself around her twice and rocked her like a child. Aria buried her face in Penn's chest like she had wanted to do in the summer when they met. She drew a huge breath and then she started to cry. She was so happy he was alive and that they were in each other's arms. The girl who never wept, cried in Reagan Airport in front of God and the world. For once she felt like she was where she was supposed to be and "home" was there in the airport, enveloped in huge arms of a man she met only once before. This second time she met him in a little southern town called Washington.

CHAPTER THIRTEEN

They retrieved Aria's luggage and Penn wouldn't let her carry anything heavy. Customarily, she was stubborn as hell and always was responsible for her own luggage and never played helpless. But today she let him carry it for her. She felt decidedly female and she liked it. This man was actually strong enough to be her man. What a revelation.

Penn escorted Aria to his car, secretly hoping that she would love it. The car was her favorite color and it was fast and classic and sexy, like a Steve McQueen movie. Aria's dad had educated her to Steve Mc Queen so she understood the gesture of the dead sexy classic car. The romance, the spirit. She was so turned on. Penn still did not know how much she loved classic cars. This was no brand new wind tunnel vehicle, it had style, substance, elegance and grace, like Penn. He deposited her in the shotgun seat and she put a scarf on her head. They looked like a magazine cover. They belonged together. They blasted down the highway, the real deal and the baby throwback. Thirty minutes later they pulled into the parking garage downtown. Penn promptly argued with the valets because no one but him was parking his car.

Aria went inside and registered and got the room. Penn arrived in the lobby and they took the elevator up to their floor. They got inside and made chit chat and Aria tried to defuse the sexual tension while they both unpacked and marveled at the sexiness and comfort of the room.

It was her taste and different for him, it was hot. Mostly he was just comfortable as hell with her. He emptied his pockets and plugged in his devices, slowly they got rid of all the trappings of daily life, they drew the curtains and locked the door. Slowly the clothes started coming off and got draped over chairs, the point was to make time stop, to forget that whatever time they had would eventually come to an end. The other goal was to close their outside lives out, to live only in this blissful, frightening, and sacred time. Getting naked in the shower was her goal. Flying always made her feel scuzzy. Subjected to the bugs of the masses, she wanted to be clean again and Aria wanted to take Penn with her into the shower while she did it.

He didn't know if they would sleep together but he ached for her. When Aria looked at Penn and said she felt gross and needed to shower, he immediately pulled off his shirt. She smiled and walked towards him and took his hand letting him know that even though they were both nervous as hell, that this was what they had both anticipated. Penn held her and she told him how tired she was because last night she was just too excited to sleep. She asked him if after the shower would he be adverse to laying down for a while, before they went to find food and water. Penn was all over it and would have done anything he could to get Aria into bed, even if it might take a little while. He just wanted to hold her close to him naked, he didn't care where or when.

If they got to have sex that would be a bonus. Penn thought they might have sex, but he knew by the time they got out of the shower, that they would be making love when it was game on, not having sex. This revelation was quite shocking to him because it happened immediately. It was already so hot between them that they both were doing their best to slow it down. Both of them were so worried about getting burned. They both knew that once they did have sex that there was no going back. They knew the experience would be so intense that everything would change forever and they would still have to work together, despite their sexual escapades, things would get very complicated after that. The funky marble bathroom took on a warm sensuality from the steam from the shower being way too hot. They turned to liquid in each other's arms, and had their first deep, long, hot, naked wet kiss, the kind of kiss that makes a lifetime and sextuplets simultaneously.

They were hot and melted and they just wanted to get clean and get into the crisp white sheets. With ninety nine percent of their defenses down, they felt better. Penn grabbed a towel, while Aria slipped into the white, plush, Turkish robe and wrapped a towel around her head.

They emerged from the bathroom, and Penn pushed her up against the outside wall and kissed her, again. Aria wrapped her lithe body around as much of this huge man as she could fit and kissed him back, alternately hard and soft. It was becoming apparent that they were the kind of couple that other people would loathe in public; it was obvious they were happy, blissfully happy, and hot for each other all at the same time. It wasn't just the animal magnetism between them; it was the blossoming of a love affair that transcends time and comprehension. They never should have been together in the first place, but they were. Strong as steel and delicate as paper. The kiss ended and Aria took Penn's hand and led him to the bed. She pulled back the duvet and they snuggled up together and laid in each others arms. They chatted and tried to calm their nerves, fawning over each other's bodies, every square inch for several hours. They went slowly; the scents, the textures, constantly touching, she rubbed and kissed and licked, bit and tickled him within an inch of his life. They reveled in it. Both of them finally felt safe in each other's arms and no one was being hunted by bad guys trying to kill Penn in Pakistan.

Penn and Aria were so relieved that the pressure was finally off and they were so exhausted that they fell asleep first, knowing damn well that they would be making hot monkey love for the rest of their lives. Because both of them never wanted to go anywhere else and they had both found the only bed that either was interested in being in ever again.

Frankly, as hot as that was it scared Penn to death, but he knew it was right. It was Mr. & Mrs. Smith on steroids. Aria fell asleep in his arms with her head on his chest like a baby. She had never allowed anyone that visual. But this was different and she slept hard and deep unlike ever before. Penn slept like he had not in years; he never relaxed in the field, it was an occupational hazard. They were so alike, it was amusing to them. Many times they would just look at each other and roll their eyes and giggle; all this from two people who were universally perceived as casual acquaintances who were also thought to be total hard asses. Together Penn and Aria were lighter than air and buffered and protected each other constantly. They made each other laugh like three year olds. Together they managed to accomplish things that neither one had been able to do individually.

The Company called three times already and Aria bugged Penn to answer the phone. He didn't want to; he wanted to be left alone. But his superiors knew damn well where he was. Back at home base he had spoken to Marshal and few close friends about the mystery girl and everyone knew he had high hopes. Everyone had figured that the sex would be wicked hot, just from what they knew about the way both of these people interacted already, everyone was curious about Penn's latest sexual toy.

Back at Langley, other spooks that he worked with expected to at least hear about very hot sexual escapades. But in the coming days the crew would be seriously disappointed. Penn found himself wanting to protect Aria and not wanting to cheapen what they were moving toward by telling everyone what was going on. This was no tart like he was used to; this was his best case scenario and he would kill anyone who tried to stand in his way. It was crystal clear to him for the very first time, she was going to belong to him if he had anything to say about it at all. Penn was used to getting what he wanted the world over, so he never had a question about his abilities. The next three days went by way too quickly, and they were inseparable. They existed in a drunken like stupor, a floaty existence that took them from the bed to the bathroom to different ethnic restaurants around the capital. For all practical purposes the rest of the world didn't even exist. They could have cared less they were absorbed in their own reality. For two people keenly aware at all times of what was going on around them, they were way out of their comfort zone on every level. It was probably the longest duration in history since the start of their relationship that news and cell phones had been turned off or just ignored. On the last morning, Penn bolted out of bed in the pre–dawn hours to listen to his voicemails and to and place some calls. Aria stirred because she had no idea why he would leave their bed at such an hour.

Penn was getting updates about his upcoming field trip. Aria decided it was okay and recalled that they had been pretty wicked the night before, so she let him tend to his business. By the time he returned forty five minutes later, she was fully awake. Aria hated being left like that and she felt raw, vulnerable and she didn't like it.

Today they would have to go their separate ways and she was freaking out about what would happen. They had already agreed last night to get together in Miami in a few weeks, but that was so far away. Penn was already in the middle of a full scale freak out. He was visibly upset at the idea of leaving Aria. He had been on the phone to associates for an hour, and he did not tell her that he had to leave early. He just panicked and broke it to her that he would be leaving in a few hours. He was running...

How could just bolt like that, after what they had shared over the last three days? They were in such a safe place and nothing in the world could compare with how they felt since they met, nothing. She was perplexed because she knew Penn felt it too; he told her so. The hours flew and when the time came she walked him down to the garage and watched him drive away. Her heart sank. She wondered how she could have allowed herself to let someone in so deep only to have him run away so quickly. Broken hearted and stuck in DC alone, she would spend the next 24 hours contemplating his odd behavior.

He left her a day early and that was a trick she had never seen before. She went back upstairs and called a friend, who tried to make her feel better. Then she attempted to run many miles on the treadmill. She pouted the entire time. She then walked up the street and got food to take back to the room. She almost passed out on the street from three days of virtually no sleep and her level of distress. She would have given almost anything to be able to fly back home that day to her beach where she belonged, instead of having to spend a night alone in their bed. She could smell Penn on everything.

Their bed, their towels, their pillowcases and it was breaking her heart again and again. She hated herself for putting her guard down enough to let him hurt her so much.

When Penn called her later she told him she could not believe what he had done. She told him flat out. He told her that while driving he realized he was afraid and realized that he had messed up badly and that he knew he had hurt her. He apologized and promised that it would never happen again. He also asked if she would agree to see him, if he came to see her on the beach. She forgave him and said yes. But what she wanted to tell him was that she was dying to see him anywhere or anytime. Instead, all she told him was that she loved him. The next day, Aria had to fly home. Penn had to get his butt into the office and pretend that the past three days never happened and that he gave a damn about his day job; just so he could focus. Good luck with that big guy, he thought to himself.

CHAPTER FOURTEEN

They both did what they had to do in order to get through the next few weeks. Penn got updates daily from the home office and took many prep trips. He talked to Aria everyday, and now they had something to build on and although they never made love in DC and had only fooled around, they were pair bonded. They already thought of themselves as a couple that had several decades under their belts. Penn couldn't wait to get through this next field trip quickly, get back to debrief, get on a plane and fly to Aria and he wanted to convince her that sleeping with him would not be a mistake. He was attempting to let her know that he would not be running away again. On this trip, he would meet her family. How weird he thought. But Aria wanted to push his face into it big time, and he understood why. So Penn was going to treat it as a learning experience and use it as a chance to gleen more personal information about the girl he had fallen in love with.

Recon, that's how he would treat the whole experience. She was at the airport to pick him up in a short, hot looking dress that looked like Warhol threw up all over it. She smelled like Palm Beach high end and absolutely perfect for him; certainly different than the girl dressed all in black in Washington who looked like she jumped out of a Japanamation Anime sequence. This girl was many girls all rolled into one. She was her own breed, unique.

Weeks before, after leaving Aria, Penn ended up on a transport following some bad guys after stints in Israel and Yemen. He wound up flying to Russia where he would be escorted almost everywhere he went. He wasn't under house arrest, but the KGB was there among the people in his fray and it was virtually impossible to tell who was who. These guys were all old school KGB style goons. Badly dressed and full of themselves; smelling of Russian pickles, borscht, whores, cheap cologne and vodka. It was as if they never got the message that the wall had come down. It was still game on to them and their supreme commander liked to kill, hit and poison people world wide to get his rocks off. Penn had long thought he had a major Napoleon complex and now he was sure of it. The man was so short, he was basically a Randy Newman song. He must have always had to pay for sex. Turns out Aria's assertion was mostly correct. He would have paid for everything, if he wasn't in the power position. Still, the Lilliputian leader had often paid in one way or another to make a genetic deposit. He was no stranger to the drill.

Penn was escorted from this perfect little town on the sea by creepy, fat ass guys who had only a few things on their minds. There was an unwritten list in every KGB guy's mind: one was the Motherland, the second was vodka, the third was where the next piece of ass was coming from, and not necessarily in that order.

The Goon Squad took him to many locations around the country to observe the manufacture of weapons systems which he was supposed to be reporting on. Showing off for the visiting journalist was a treat. Screwing with his head and fucking up his body might be even more fun, including getting him drunk and laid. What they didn't know was that Penn was there on a prepared agenda whether they liked it or not. It wasn't the same one the Russian weapons manufacturer and Moscow had in mind. Penn was supposed to cover what the Russian government, which is (aka the KGB) had given the green light to. It was supposed to look like he had the approvals of the companies he was visiting, so he could be used for propaganda purposes. His role to play was to be wined and dined in a government bugged dacha for six nights and pretend that he actually drank non- stop... just like they did. Fat chance; he never would willingly.

This made for a great deal of operational creativity, as Penn looked for places to put the vodka. Creative imbibing, napkins, plants, seat cushions, anything. He needed to put it anywhere, except inside his body where it would impair him. One night after the day's driving and work, they had a reception in his honor and showed off the local custom. It was complete with everything a good spy party should have. Food, locals, location, KGB, vodka, chicks, government folk and whores.

All Penn wanted to do was leave this bullshit commie party and get loose into the little town up the way, avoid being followed and find a safe place where he could call Aria. Anyplace would work, a restaurant that wasn't bugged, or maybe a side street. But instead, he would have to settle for hanging out at this party for now and looking for a place to put the vodka he had pouched in the side of his cheek. He motioned that he was going to the bathroom and spit it at point blank range into some heavy draperies while on his way to the bathroom. One other night he spit on to the floor and stepped in it when the two ghouls he was stuck with were preoccupied with a piece of ass.

In this part of the world, all currency of social and business activity revolved around a piece of ass 24/7. Penn was offered girls every night at every event. He knew that girls who showed up uninvited to his room every night were maybe his daughter's age and some were in their early teens. But they were all potential assassins. Most were victims entrapped in the Russian sex slave trade, snatched from all over the world. These girls, if they did not die in the initial trauma, wished they were dead. They were just regular girls, never to be seen or heard from by their families again, they were disappeared behind the real iron curtain, the real one that never fell. Only naive westerners and people in Washington believed that the cold war was over.

They were all drug addicted and HIV positive, and there to kill him one way or another. He had been warned in advance by the home office and had no intention of screwing around. Penn had one girl he wanted and she wasn't in Russia, she was home a stones throw from the Caribbean where the water was azure blue and the dolphins jumped in the sunshine.

Penn was entrenched, and this was another situation involving some pretty nasty dogs hanging around a really nice Dascha in the Russian countryside. Dogs always seemed to be around when Penn was present. It was a good thing that dogs, even bad guys dogs seemed to like him. Bad guys seem to always have guard dogs, not just for security but also for image. They seem to always want to control their press, and with the internet things seemed to be worse than ever. It was akin to a big bad guy handbook that they got issued when they became a full–fledged bad guy. Step one: Buy a few really scary big dogs. Step two: Make sure you sleep in a really creepy looking dark place with lots of old ratty Persian rugs and really expensive looking shit in it. You must complete step one and two before you're allowed to go on to step three through five. Step three: acquire largest pair of expensive black sunglasses available and live in them.

Step four: make people come to you and Step five: make sure you get a trophy girlfriend now that you can afford to buy one. Treat females in general like chattel. That was the drill of this pack of sexually diseased, drunk and dysfunctional people walking around that looked like extras in the Underworld movie series. End of story. The time that Penn was stuck in Russia wore on, and it was immensely taxing. He was over the people and so he opted out of dressing like a vampire. Of course constantly being watched was difficult and "bor-ing" and after a few nights the spy romance had worn off and things were starting to get "sticky." Penn's hosts were starting to look at him suspiciously. It was getting harder to get the mission done. He had to be calm cool and collected every single minute of every day. Solid under pressure. Langley knew his success rates and they knew that they could count on Penn in a world where you can't count on anything. But even great spies get into unavoidability tight and supremely dangerous situations. It gets to be part of the job at a certain level and Penn had become a permanent resident. One night it got to be a little "too nuts," and he thought they had made him for sure. He was positive that his hosts had figured out his mission was and he could not have that. But he was out there all alone in "BFE" in Russia on the Black Sea with no backup. Just some wild ass friendly locals who knew the drill and they were ours… for decades. They were in… as deep as deep gets.

Deep inside enemy territory for years, these guys knew everything about everybody. One night it so got intense that Penn was sure would not be alive by morning. He had to get away that night and managed to make it up the road to the friendly locals. Penn and the guys were sitting around after he got out, trying to eat and prepping to leave when they got a crazy phone call and a tip from the home office. The group at the table thought they were safe and a step ahead of the game but, the call revealed that they were anything but. When the home office called Penn thought it was a sick joke, and everyone at the table thought it was too. But the guy who took the phone call turned sheet white and looked at Penn. He said, "We have to get you out of here now." The comment took a moment to land. Only then did everyone realize that they were in danger. The KGB had made Penn, they knew his true identity, and they were coming to kill him.

The group of men left immediately for an abandoned airstrip. Enroute, Penn was introduced to an ex Turkish fighter pilot who was dressed as a civilian and had an unmarked 2 seat F 16 trainer at his disposal. There was a whole squadron based at the airstrip, hidden in plain sight. The pilot flew by Braille lightless by moonlight, literally below the radar. Somewhere over Eastern Europe they picked up some friendly NATO escort jets and quietly they deposited Penn and his unlikely chauffer on to one of our bases in Europe.

"The Langley Guys" were waiting for them and only then did they learn that the Russians scrambled two Sukhoi Fighters and had orders to shoot down the F 16. Earlier Penn had no idea that the evening would be so action packed. All he was focused on was getting out of the storybook looking little town on the Black Sea. Now, he was in a country that wasn't even on the radar four hours ago… "But hey my butt is in one piece," he thought. Hell, he had barely gotten out of Israel which was safe, and Yemen which was not, much less Russia with his ass in one piece before he started freaking out about needing to speak to Aria. Things were on his mind, specifically upcoming field trips. But this was not the trip that bothered him. The trips that bothered him were the trips that were coming up. He wanted to speak to her about his thoughts, which had been violent, vivid and frightening. These were going to make Israel, Yemen and Russia look like kindergarten banter. There were many things flying around in his head, and he knew that he was also going to have to answer some of Aria's questions. At this point he had to decide if he would be making her aware of some of his upcoming missions. Penn had many things he wanted to tell her, but because it was still so new, there were only a few things that he actually could share. Operational security and his movements could never be divulged. Most things he could never tell her. But she knew this already.

But he felt for some reason that she had a handle on his psyche much better than he had a handle on her's. Part of the reason for this trip was to test the theory. What did she really know about him? Did she really know what he did, and if so, how could she? But she seemed to know almost everything. If she understood, would she still love him? Would she still lay in his arms and make love with him knowing what those hands had also been responsible for? It scared him to death. The thought that she may not be able to deal with it... because he could not fall and then find out that she couldn't hack the ride. Seemingly no one else was able to do away with him, though his enemies continued to try daily. But this hundred–pound Lara Croft anineme was a real threat.

They were going to have to do some serious talking this week– as well as make love for the first time. No pressure... no pressure at all. The next few days came off without too much of a hitch, there were little bits of drama. Like when Penn had to go marching out front to the desk because some ridiculous cocktail waitress all but threw a drink in Aria's face and hit on Penn in front of her, twice. He was so upset that she kept treating Aria so badly that he asked for another waitress because this one was so out of bounds. He bound up front to the manager because Aria was so hurt. He wanted her to know that he loved her and that he had not hit on the bimbo that had come on to him before in front of her.

The woman was just a bitch like so many women, and she looked to humiliate Aria and take her man. She didn't count on Aria putting up a fight or a man knowing where he wanted to be. Penn worked to gain Aria's trust and after a while... a long while it worked. Penn met Aria's parents and that was successful and strange. Having to pretend that they didn't just make love for the first time or walk down the beach in the moonlight digging their toes in the sand. That they weren't just like a sappy love song or a piece of prose or a Shakespeare play was so very difficult. They were just people who worked together on projects that no one really understood.

It was amazing that Aria's father never knew. Actually, he probably did know, he was just in denial because he didn't want to have to deal emotionally with a relationship like that. Aria was sure that it had something to do with being sensible, and being born in the Midwest. Aria took Penn everywhere and showed him all that she could around her stomping grounds in the short period of time they were together. Forcing themselves to get out of bed given the amount of work, play, meetings and sex that had to be tended to was not easy but somehow they managed. It was always an uphill battle. Then the day came when Aria had to put Penn back on an airplane and he left that little beach in South Florida and that girl standing on it. But this time she cried because she was happy, not sad, and they had a date to rendezvous again in Washington, assuming of course that he survived his next mission to the "Sandbox."

CHAPTERFIFTEEN

He was headed to Pakistan again and it was a tall order for him to come back in one piece, but she believed in him and in herself. Above all there was one fact that they both believed in, that there was nothing they couldn't do for the good of the country if they only they did it together.

In short order Penn was back on the ground getting entrenched in Washington and making side trips to surrounding areas to prepare for the upcoming mission as was customary. Sometimes senior handlers came to him to prepare him, sometimes he had to go to them. Such was the routine in places all over the world, places that the average person would never surmise. Little picture perfect postcard towns and coffee shops and malls literally teeming with spies in pursuit of viable, actionable, intelligence. All taking place while you shopped for underwear at Target and garden hose at Home Depot and got your latte in the drive through at Starbucks, sang karaoke and mowed your lawn and shoveled your front walk of snow. People literally did not recognize that there were spies virtually everywhere. It all happened right under everyone's noses every single day.

As Penn grew more comfortable with he an Aria's relationship he lowered his guard and would pop off about some aspects of his clandestine work while they were strolling or discussing current events; he secretly loved the fact that he had stopped needing to lie to Aria for security purposes.

Each time he slipped, Aria was struck by how people generally were so caught up in their day that most seemed completely unaware of what was actually going on in the world oblivious to the dangers that two bit delusional rulers really represent. It baffled both of them how people could be so clueless. How could voters in the U.S. elect such politicians who were fixated on little more than perpetuating their own power base and sense of self importance. American's were great, kind people. Most were just currently seriously misdirected and in massive denial thinking that the world and their government owed them everything. This ubiquitous feeling of entitlement was like a weight on the shoulders of the guys and gals in the field and it was something that was often discussed, especially in the annual psychological "check ups." Between the stress of work and the issues and lack of support at so many levels for a strong intelligence capability, Penn often wondered how true patriots in Washington managed to accomplish anything and enhance the country's security. Often times, life and death loyalty only seemed to work one way. And the current admin certainly had not been helping anything. They had been torturing clandestine for awhile with lack of support, threats of a legal nature and threatening to out agents for political gain were becoming weekly occurrences. Thankfully, it was not an issue on Penn's team so he never had to deal with directly.

There had been many successful missions over many years with Marshal's team, with Marshal serving as Penn's principle handler. One day, shortly before Penn was scheduled to perform his next mission, Marshal met Penn for lunch in a restaurant with a heavy heart. They almost always met for food, the bonding, the intimacy and Marshal loved to eat. Marshal never delivered any news good or bad by phone. Given the choice, he knew neither one of them would consider this good news. In fact, Marshal knew that both of them would be hurt by the nature of their discussion.

Of course they could handle it. After all, they were spies for fuck sake! But the news that Marshal had to share still sucked, even though they were professionals. The message that had come down from the clandestine operations directorate was that Marshal's operational status was being drastically altered. The change itself was not out of the ordinary; from time to time the agency teams expanded and people were moved based on abilities, mission, operational security and so forth. They never liked to let someone get too comfortable and they discouraged people from getting too close. It was all so counterintuitive. Unlike many soldiers who do a great deal of waiting and may not ever see combat, with spies it's game on all the time. Marshal tried to couch the jarring news that the agency was breaking up the A Team, but secretly neither one of them really bought it. Penn wondered what the hell would happen now and before he could ask his best friend Marshal told him what was up.

Penn was being reassigned for this next operational rotation to Pakistan to another handler named Clayton Bullock. Marshal had great things to say about Clay, who was the expert on this specific operation. There was absolutely no one else in the agency whose subject specific knowledge matched Clay's. He was as intimately involved as anyone was allowed to get. He knew his shit and he was legendary. For Clay, the situation was very personal and he had some major demons to exorcise. He was a freak like Marshal and Penn. Clay was the poster child for a modern upright citizen. Marshal knew all of this and despite his loss and sadness, if he was being forced to hand Penn off to someone, Clay was the only man on the team Marshal would feel comfortable entrusting his friend's life to. Clay was so vested in this operation that he would have done just about anything to ensure it's success and make sure that Penn pulled through safe. Marshal liked Clay's operational style so much that his head was actually at peace. He was basically the home base version of Penn, just not a field guy. He had the respect and admiration of everyone who worked under deep cover. He was at the top of his game and he was a straight shooter. He loved his wife; he was a decent human being working in a world that was a pile of shit. He loved humanity, he hated selfishness and he saved lives for a living.

Marshal tried to bring all these positive qualities to the table when he spoke to Penn about Clayton. It was not easy, it was never easy. No need to alarm him any more than he already would be. Pre–game changes were always nerve racking, Marshal knew this.

109

It was his job to take care of his guys, all of them. It was just different with Penn, they hung and did business outside of "The Company." They were each other's lifelong bromance. They did all the scary, fun, silly, serious stuff all over the world for years together and laughed their asses off the entire time. They were best friends and they trusted each other with their lives completely. All this care and respect took Penn back, and he was happy despite the position he was in. He was grateful to have Marshal's love and devotion. In a place like the agency where relationships like theirs were frowned upon, Penn knew he was lucky to have Marshal–his brother of another mother. Marshal knew that once you are actually in a situation you had better not be allergic to adrenaline because it's game on 24–7. Marshal, being such a passionate creature, was monumentally devastated but he would never say that aloud. Penn knew this and he was just as sad. Penn always knew who was on the other end of the phone and who to trust. Marshal was always the one pulling the levers and triggers and watching his ass from every possible angle. Marshal...Marshal was the brother he never had and what was going down sucked about as badly as a decision could suck.

Marshal broached the topic of the next field assignment which Penn would be doing. Since Marshal was being phased out and Clay was assuming the reigns it would be strange and unique for everyone involved. This next field operation would be the most dangerous Penn had ever attempted to complete. For most people it would be suicide–which was why they were giving it to him. He was quite literally, the only numbered agent licensed to kill and quite possibly the only one who could handle it. Mentally, physically and physiologically, the agency and his entire team knew that he was one of kind. The level of his operational participation had amped up greatly over the past few months and the operation's chief started coming to him with assignments they never had considered giving to anyone else. He was an animal and the game had come together for him over the past few months. He had attained a whole new level of expertise including his ability to leverage his cover and it gave him unparalleled access to places and people who never suspected his real mission. Penn's whole career was culminating now. Which was convenient because the free world never needed anyone on the side of right quite so much. Everyone on the home team noted this fact and it impacted the level of the missions that his operational team was asked to plan and participate in. The effectiveness of their unit caused the directorate to rethink and retool their positions with regard to planning and wish lists over many months as situations presented themselves.

Penn told the shrinks he had a new secret weapon and her name was Aria. It was a new ball game for everyone on the team with him. They could count on him for his cool head under any circumstances. He was unflappable. Finally he was able to control his formerly uncontrollable aggressive testosterone driven tendencies. A little bit of seasoning had been very good for Penn and so was Aria. He could really hold his shit now and he had the experience and the raw power and intelligence to back it up. Penn knew the agency was really letting their balls swing on this one. A great deal was riding on this mission so it was a moral imperative that it came off without a glitch and that it was not a repeat of a similar situation.

Everyone knew this trip back to Pakistan would make Penn's last trip look like playtime with Barney. This trip was so personal to so many people being the culmination of many previous field assignments, amassing all the intel to get one specific task accomplished. If this trip was completed successfully it would reverberate throughout the agency for eternity as payback for a heinous act that was committed years before. Everyone would know about the outcome. The day came for him to leave for the Sandbox and Penn had the pre game jitters as usual. He had done a ton of prep with Clayton and he felt confident in the new team. They trusted and liked each other.

It got comfortable quickly partly because of necessity. Clay realized what a terrible position Penn was in with Marshal's exit right before going out and he was sensitive to it. Every time a handler changed, it was a big deal that no one could ignore. Aria knew what was happening and she had a very high level of distress as she would have to go through it too, without the benefit of support. Getting used to trusting someone else, to watch out for and save her man's tail in the most horrendous of situations around the globe. Knowing that Penn was sweating it bothered her. Aria hoped that Clay was what she thought he was. Aria secretly hoped that Clay would be so wrapped up in everything, vested in the situation, and in Penn that he would never drop the ball, ever. She prayed for Clay daily and forced herself into his head and loved him like she had loved Marshal. It was important, it was Penn's survival. She needed to support Clay and he needed her support, but he never knew it.

CHAPTERSIXTEEN

Penn hit the ground running again in his favorite country in his favorite part of the world, much to his dismay. Penn got through customs, cleared out of the airport and hopped in a cab and headed for the hotel. He did not trust the cab driver so he made a quick assessment of everything around him and then took his weapon out in the backseat of the cab and hid it between his legs. From the minute the cab pulled out of the airport Penn was assaulted by everything Pakistan. The steaming searing heat, the smells and sights really bothered him this time. He still had a bad taste in his mouth from months before when an insect tried to end his life. The cab was filthy and so were the surroundings. The cab belched blue exhaust fumes. The taxi stopped at multiple traffic lights and there were dirty broken down old cars everywhere Penn looked. Scooters and people filled the streets; it was overwhelming. With every stop that slowed them to a crawl, Penn felt like they had parked and his anxiety mounted. Penn kept flashing back to a bad experience in Afghanistan and a suicide bomber he encountered. The cab driver could be sitting on a serious amount of plastic explosives ready to take himself out with the white American in the back seat. Even more poetic would be stopping in traffic and being surrounded by all these jalopies and scooters as someone walks up to the car intent on another hit on Penn.

He hated feeling this kind of lack of control. Months before he had been shot in the chest at point blank range and some experiences just have to change you. Getting shot in the chest is one of them. He had not realized how shocked he was or that he had not processed the experience completely until he was back on the ground, this day in Pakistan. But he was feeling it now. He rubbed his pistol trying to comfort himself. Penn knew full well his usual weapon of choice would not save his ass if there were any plastic explosives nearby. He tried to banish such crazy thoughts, but that was the thing, the thoughts weren't crazy because these things really did happen regularly anywhere in the world there were terrorists, more specifically Islamic terrorists. Penn thought it must be ridiculous to be part of a fanatical religious community hell bent on death and mayhem. You would think that with all the Muslims on the planet that they would function more like Japanese society. By putting social pressure on the bad apples and enforcing consequences upon their violent brethren who despoiled everyone else in the faith. Surely they could affix some social consequences for reprehensible behavior to alter such conduct. This premise has successfully worked with different races from across the globe for thousands of years, so why didn't they do it?

Crazy idea, but Penn thought it just might be worth a shot. This trip would be high profile and it was something the agency was counting on, at least partly to help keep his butt intact. It was no guarantee, but it might actually help. The low-lifes might be less apt to try to annihilate someone whom they felt would be watched, escorted and valuable to their cause. These groups are nothing if not opportunistic. They are not necessarily good at capitalizing on it; although they as a group had been getting much better at doing so lately. Since 9 /11 the groups both named and unnamed had looked towards their CNN moments. They look for the biggest bang for their terrorist buck. They look for the journalist that either doesn't get it, hates the West or is looking to make a name for themself. "Capitalizing on sensational media had become a function of necessity for the bad guys manipulating the naive West but some of us, thank God, knew better and had finally started responding accordingly." "It took us too damn long, but we were finally getting better at fighting their dirty asymmetrical war. We were learning to communicate better agency to agency, sharing more information and getting to our end game faster. It was a good thing because basically it was one of our only trump cards."

Penn thought it was always so ridiculous because here we were fighting a war world–wide that no one group could see or was responsible for. A war entirely financed on both sides by America and the rest of the West with it's need for oil and now with the current administration standing in the way of all domestic development we were choking off our only shot at a healthy, effective path to support energy, jobs and national security.

By failing to sharply curb it's appetite for imported crude oil, the West was helping to underwrite the terrorists' monetary stash to commit mass murder world wide. It was tragic and brutal. The development of domestic energy would have changed the balance significantly, but the base of the current White House prevented that from happening. Penn hunkered down at the hotel, unpacked both his bags and kissed his kevlar. He called Clayton back at Langley. Penn had to get some more input on his local contacts and get any updates on the threats that he could be facing. He checked in to make sure everything was running according to the operational schedule and let Clay know that he was okay. After a quick shower and a few hours of sleep, he left for his first meeting. It was the last hurrah for hot summer weather in Pakistan and desert hot is a whole different kind of hot. The shower with semi clean water was a huge coo. On this mission he would basically be operating solo. There would be people close by to clean up the messes when he was finished doing what needed to be done. Technically, he had backup when he needed it, though they could never be seen together there would be people around just in case. Everyone had to be very careful though, because these were all "in country" people and they were buried very deep. Their covers, like Penn's, could not afford to be blown. Because unlike Penn, they would not have the option to leave the country when the operation wrapped up.

Penn had never met and worked with the station chief but he was a friend of Clay's. It bothered Penn that he really didn't know him. He wished he could have been close with him at the time of the op. But he trusted Clay implicitly and if Clay said that he was a real guy, that was good enough for him. Penn knew he might have a chance to develop a personal relationship with the station chief later in the year. It seemed as though he was always in the Sandbox in one way or another. Every time he had some time off and ended up in a more civilized place; the agency just kept pulling him back in by his short and curlies. The local field agents were always in serious jeopardy during these kinds of operations. An experienced and skilled station chief made all the difference here. It would be important that the locals stayed safe and hidden in plain sight. It was a tall order. Their tasks were very difficult and senior officers were always amazed after they wrapped an operation, especially back at headquarters. There was always that blissed out, crazy high afterwards that no one else had a hope in hell of understanding. It was almost giddy. They would hang and drink and eat and talk shit together whenever they could. Bound by extreme circumstances in a foreign land. But they never allowed themselves to get smug… no matter how daring a mission they pulled off.

No normal people would ever believe you anyway. Regular people would always think you were full of shit and the bigger the deal and the more dangerous it was the less regular people would ever believe it. Penn's team became masters at being on the receiving end of the disapproving eye rolls. You pretty much never got any down time from the work or the judgments. Within the groups or outside in your real life. CIA officers working in the clandestine branch under cover rarely got a chance to relax, but when it happened they loved it. It was always easiest when you were with other members of the brotherhood. There was nothing like sharing that life on the line camaraderie that very few people on the planet understand.

All the meetings went as planned, and Penn followed all the steps to the Nth degree, that he was supposed to track for this operational sequence to be correct. Part of it was the complexity of the mission, part of it the emotion of the players and the light that years of new intel had shed on the situation. The amount of intelligence made this mission unique. Once it was done it would never have to be revisited. It would bring closure and everyone who was allowed to know was rooting for Penn and Clay and the whole ops team. "Shit, everyone was so jacked among the few that were privy to the pre–op intel and briefings that if they could have taken out a full page ad in Stars and Stripes and The Washington Post they would have." This time everyone just knowing the agency was doing the right thing and settling a score, would have to be enough. They could not afford a pre–op slip up or any misstep that could tip off the bad guys and let them know that the good guys were coming to eat their babaghanoush.

There would be two main meetings to facilitate two hits. Two. Penn turned over the number in his head again and again trying to wrap his mind around it. The best case scenario would be eradication of the rest of vermin in the world. But heck everyone is entitled to their fantasies. But today's job was two, the others would be taken care of in due course. Penn wanted to make sure that the others were taken to completion as well. It bothered him but he knew that was not his job or his call, but he wished it was. He knew what everyone wanted to do. He would have been happy to have his team be the delivery boys on that one. Everyone was waiting for the day and when that day came it would completely close the book. They all dreamt about it, especially Clay. This operation would be the biggest and most important undertaken by anyone to date and this would open the flood gates for the wrap up with the past. Penn would have loved to be a part of the last operation in order to make sure everyone had a poker buddy when they got to hell, but he also knew that it would have to wait. He got past his day dream only because he needed to focus on the task at hand.

His belly and his head hungered for food and that restaurant where he'd been a couple of times before where he had that great bowtie pasta in a light cream sauce.

CHAPTERSEVENTEEN

By the time Penn was installed in Karachi the second time, Aria was feeling very confident in her ability to connect with him. Still, it was very intense and Aria, just like Penn, looked forward to when he wasn't in the field as that was the only time she was able to see him and mellow out. When he was safe, and with her she had the luxury of thinking about things other than the degree of craziness triggered by some dictator or sociopath who lived thousands of miles away. Real problems, not the simple problems that most folks here in the States deal with daily. Life and death for the world on a grand scale. Death, destruction and mayhem, not kids skateboarding on the sidewalk, underage drinking and some credit card debt. Penn had already spent a great deal of time on the phone with Clay. Penn checked in with his local CIA station chief. He always made it a priority to get an update on the threat environment wherever he went so he knew what he might be facing. He also talked to his local contacts and connected with anyone Clay told him could be useful. Clay was known for his relationships throughout the world, which was part of the reason he was such a great handler. Clay was tight with the station chief in Pakistan even though Penn only knew him in passing. Penn had spoken to media people in country before he arrived, because the Company had wanted this to be a high profile visit. For this reason he went out of his way to identify himself as a journalist on assignment in Pakistan.

That also made him an even bigger target, but the visibility might help him in what everyone needed to accomplish and it bolted up nicely to his real job. Penn felt uneasy about the whole trip. What bothered him the most wasn't the mission itself, but who could he really trust. The biggest danger was the double agents and opportunists that could be flipped for money and since it was always life and death in one of the third worlds shitholes, it didn't take very much to alter someone's alliances.

Joint operations were common. The State Department, the White House and the Pentagon loved them. There had been more in the past few years, and it produced some successes, but the risks were always greater. You could never know who was really on your side, and command, control and communications was always a serious issue. It could get very dangerous very quickly not knowing who your familials were. To help mitigate the risk, Penn's team went to great lengths to identify the bad guys. You never wanted to be caught with your ass hanging out. Penn and his fellow operatives were laser focused, they had drilled for a full blown mission like this repeatedly. Tunnel vision... it was a moral imperative in order to get it done correctly and get out alive. But no matter how much they trained and prepared, Penn was always amazed at how different things could be when it came time to execute. There were always some people who knew what he was really there to do, but overall not many people did.

As Penn rose through the ranks with higher level clearance his operational teams got smaller, more targeted and then black. Things went from grey and hazy to so charcoal that you could not see anything at all. Operations of this nature were not typical and many were not run through normal channels, chiefly for the safety of those involved. These were bought and paid for, run out of a myriad of secure and basically secret and unknown underground locations around the U.S. and overseas. Run out of someplace, any place and places that no one would ever know about. It didn't matter ... none of these secure operating locations existed anyhow. You could do more with less because of technology. The differences in the technology from even 10 or 20 years ago were mind blowing and it made all the difference in the world in what a team could handle quickly and with minimal personnel. The less people involved the better. As Penn took on more responsibility over the months he became more concerned with leaks. With Clay, it had become wildly important and even though Penn had a "den mother" that tracked his location regardless of where he was in the world, the concept of a smaller more secure team gave him and his fellow operatives engaged in assignments the world over some necessary mental relief.

Penn thought for all the trouble that Clay and some of the other guys had gone to on this one it was unlike anything he had ever seen in the operational arena. It made him feel more confident, if that was possible. To feel more confident about what was basically a ballsy second attempt at a now infamous suicide mission in the bowels of Pakistan, was priceless. He expected to have almost no time eat on this mission and every minute would be accounted for. He would have to schedule time to use the facilities. Getting in and out with his head attached to his shoulders would be another trick, not just getting the job done. Serving as live bait sucked, but somebody had to do it. No problem, no problem at all "a walk in the park, my ass."

Now that Penn was planted in the hotel room and had talked multiple times to Clay he reached out for his local mole. Penn was after a specific guy and the operation wouldn't work with out his cooperation. After repeated tries he made contact. Like his predecessor, Penn was the "journalist." This time however he was determined to avoid the same fate that had befallen his now deceased colleague in this 21st century holy war. The mole never knew what hit him. He never suspected he was being used. Operational Hazard... Whoops. Penn unpacked the rest of his carry on gear and the suitcases. He was digging for some of the food he managed to smuggle in to the country. He had pepperoni, crackers and cheese, protein bars and candy. It wasn't exactly a gourmet meal but at least it would keep him alive and allow him to avoid any of the local food for the next 48 hours. Penn would only be in Pakistan 48 hours, only 2 days on the ground.

The execution of every move had to be precise and there was a very strict ops plan. Screw-ups, no matter how minor, were not an option. During the planning stages of the operation there had been talk of escaping following the mission over the border. Someone suggested getting smuggled out in the back of a vehicle, but Penn knew enough about such schemes to know that more often than not they ended disastrously. He would have no part of it. It's always much easier to come up with an escape plan when it's not your ass in the line of fire. All the same, they also had an abort plan if the shit hit the fan in a big bad ugly way, but after a certain point he and his team would be committed. If things went very wrong he would milk the journalist cover to the hilt. Not that the strategy saved his former team member. Penn knew full well that he would be walking a guide wire at a high altitude in very windy conditions with no safety net.

Within a couple of hours of his arrival, Penn made a bee line for the local CIA operating base, to check in with the station chief so he could get a visual. Penn was cleared and was admitted access. He was buzzed through and came in to the lobby and Chamberlin's first in command got sent down to the lobby to pick him up.

Chamberlin's guy was different than any of the support personnel you usually encounter in the field. At home, these operatives would be dressed. But in the Middle East you had to dress comparatively shabby to avoid being an operational hazard. Making yourself or your teammates a target for your vanity was definitely not an option.

Standing out was a problem waiting to happen–it was like ringing the jihadie dinner bell. The station chief, Chamberlin Forester, was a tall guy, probably an ex operative and a lifer. Smart, polished, focused, sensitive and aware. One of the survivors, he was somewhere around 60, a friend of Clays and he knew where every single body was buried. That in itself was amazing because in this part of the world there were so few people that had any real history and there were so many bodies buried. Chamberlin was savvy to all the players on every side. This made him valuable. He was also a very even keel in an extremely hot headed part of the world. Penn was aware of this and was happy as hell to have him as an ally. Penn imagined that Chamberlin knew everyone and their mother back at the home office and he probably knew the guys, who knew the guys. Everyone knew that "those guys" knew all of the history. They had been "in" since they were kids and every last one of them really knew what was going on, they had seen it all and they were fascinating to speak with.

Some of them had actually started out in mailrooms back in the day and had worked under many administrations. They all knew each other, and there were only a handful of them left and they founded what amounted to a private club. Penn, knowing all of this hoped that he would have more of a relationship with Chamberlin in the future. While at Chamberlin's office, Penn had a video conference with Clay and picked up the most current intel from the Israelis, the French and MI 6. There were a few addendums but no issues to speak of. Primary targets of opportunity that comprised different parts of the same puzzle protecting national security and the GWOT (global war on terrorism), in military parlance. It was always interesting to see who had which pieces... who would share and the Israelis by nature usually had the most overlapping details with us. Penn got use of an empty conference room for the day which allowed him to make secure calls to Clay and some junior assistant to Chamberlin kept Penn in constant supply of food and water. The table in front of him was strewn with papers and remnants of all types of food making it look like a small woodland creature had taken up temporary residence. With all the Intel Penn had to get through he needed a steady stream of nutrition to counter the extreme jet lag and time difference. He kept forgetting, "Yeah, I just got here, today." Eating with one hand and working with the other, he did Massad intel first, since it tended to be fresher.

Both countries were always balls to the wall 24 / 7 and people died regularly trying to attain the unattainable. Because they knew that there was always that one piece of intel that would make a real difference. The average American will never know how many people in different places have sacrificed themselves to help save humanity for another day. "The unaware" just get the benefit of another smile, a sunrise, a breath.

Most of the rest of the first day for Penn was spent at the office setting up meetings and following up for the umpteenth time with the contacts and putting all the pieces in order. What Penn and Clay did daily was akin to moving chess pieces 24 hours a day and the world was a giant board. The pieces were constantly moving and they tried their best to think three moves ahead, even though it seemed that they floated around the board with no rhyme or reason in real time. But this was no game, there were no rules and no stopping. The only thing that would stop "the play" was death, which is the debt that Penn was sent there to collect on anyway.

CHAPTER EIGHTEEN

Aria was doing all the research in between work, and learning things about people and the agencies that a lot of the guys who were in now didn't even know… the history of the clandestine services, the who and where…the remarkable people who had given some, if not, all of their lives, to the service in defense of the country, of Americans and of the Free World. It calmed her to know these things and to fill her head with the stability of the past of the people who had come before them. Before their unique life, and love, inside and outside the agency. She found unlikely players even famous people, all bona fide heroes and regular people who had blazed the path of self–sacrifice long before them. All to preserve our freedoms and contain or annihilate the world's most dangerous people and situations. It revved her engines just to connect with these ghosts, because at least then she could feel that she and Penn were not really out there all alone. The lone wolf set out looking for her wolf pack, then she met Penn and everything came together. Aria strapped on a piece and became part of "The Wild Bill Wolf Pack". All the way around it was a match made in heaven. The alone, but not quite alone thing, seemed to be just what Penn and Aria ordered. For the first time in both of their lives, they were both definitely not alone. They were together, they had each other. They understood each other, and thankfully the agency seemed to be enlightened enough after a while that they got it. Their response in the end surprised everyone, including Penn.

Penn had done all he could do at the office for the day and tomorrow would be the operational day. Today the goal was to find a place to eat and then crash so he could be up before the crack of dawn to prep for one hell of a day. He said his good byes at the station and as he was making his way across the lobby he bumped into a friend; another agent that he was stationed with in Europe earlier in his career. Neither one had any idea that the other was in Karachi. At first they barely acknowledged each other to avoid drawing any attention. They made their way back into a safe area of the building and promptly dropped the cover and formality. A big hello and a big hug that only spending time with someone that you're real tight with when your ass is in a sling provides. Penn lit up like a Christmas tree and so did Mike McCarthy. Mike was from Boston and spent the beginning of his career training to lose his thick New England accent. Unlike most Massachusetts residents, Mike was a Republican and he did not miss that about home. He wanted the government the hell out of his personal life and never made any bones about telling people where to put it if they tried to control or intrude on his personal space. This straight–forward manner and independence is what Penn loved most about Mike. Zero tolerance for bullshit, and he always told the truth. You always knew where you stood when Mike was around. Penn never knew that Marshal had been Mike's handler as well before the handoff.

When the friends saw each other it was if they had not spent years apart in and out of Washington at basically different as well as some of the same times. Not being allowed to keep operational tabs on each other was always hard on close friends. "Within The Company things had become so compartmentalized after 9/11 for security purposes that tracking and /or finding anyone with whom you were not directly involved operationally had become a matter of state." It was a total pain in the ass. It impeded everyone's communication. That coupled with the internet took away even more of the personal in your face trust that is the backbone of operatives in the field. Often it's a matter of life and death. Everyone had become so afraid to speak to anyone else. Though everyone knew this was the way it had to be, no one liked it very much. All of the agents working in the clandestine division took every opportunity to creatively bitch about it and safely bend the rules when security was not compromised. The bottom line is that it was hard because the men and women whose lives took place in the field needed each other on and off the road. Even though they couldn't share operational details, theirs was an exclusive brotherhood. There were so few of them and everyone was almost always gone so far from home. It's a hard life that's tough to deal with, but they do. "When you see someone who is safe to speak with, who knows who you really are and you don't have to pretend, or lead a double life every minute it's comforting." Everyone knows what not to ask, it's liberating as all get out, almost restorative.

You get to pretend you live a normal existence because everyone does the same thing for a living. Everyone that is in your group gets to pretend with you. "Lets play normal" is so much fun to operatives that when they know they are going to get to do it they get excited and the group always grows. It's just like when you have an informal dinner at Langley. You're in front of your own kind and it's safe. If it's not a working dinner where you have to be "on" the whole time, you can relax and it's the next best thing to either your childhood kitchen or to your wife's kitchen.

Penn and Mike arranged a dinner for later in the day at a safe place where they would not arouse suspicion. They decided to take Chamberlin's number one guy Frank with them. Mike had known Frank for years so he was able to vouch for him with Penn. Frank and Mike would swing by Penn's hotel and pick him up in few hours. Penn insisted that it must be early. He had a big day tomorrow and he didn't want to be kept out late. He could not afford to screw this up. Not going to happen. Penn headed out from the station by a car that Chamberlin had arranged for him, a safe car, a real coup in this time and place. Penn got in safe and sound to the hotel and managed to get in a couple of hours of shut eye.

He was still new to country and only running on a few hours of sleep. He was happy that Mike had work to do so he didn't have to feel guilty about getting some sleep. That nap would save his butt tomorrow. Operatives in the field and operatives back at the home office often ran on no sleep. Even guys that were sleepers in their "real lives" got virtually no sleep in the field. It was a given maybe a few hours in a couple of days and then up all night doing crazy shit. It never changed. That in fact was probably the only part of the deal that was constant. In his real life Penn was a sleeper, he just did not know it. He could never stay down for long, he would always wake because of his belly. It woke him way before daybreak daily demanding food.

On top of the physical workload, the mental workload was as formidable. People constantly came to him for his take on every-thing...policy issues, defense, threat assessment, issues about dic-tators of the week. So with no alternative, Penn had finally gotten comfortable with this. Penn had become one of the chosen few who knew most of the facts in a computer driven world where very few people know anything other than what they can look up on Google. In fact, the exception to this rule of all people was prob-ably Aria. She was used to being in the same position as Penn.

Like Penn, Aria was a fair, stable, heady, even keel decision maker and being female and young she was a very odd duck. But she didn't mind so much once she saw that people did the exact same thing to Penn and to her father. She just took it as a com-pliment. Still, it sucked her energy being the responsible one all the time. But she tried to navigate the new waters with grace and aplomb. Aria, like Penn, was often gravely misunderstood and this caused great discomfort for her. People who met her when she was getting things done thought she was a bossy bitch or just loud. But in point of fact, the people close to her knew none of these claims were anywhere near accurate. She was the polar opposite, Aria just did not speak to hear herself or from a point of ego. She func-tioned only to serve a purpose, the girl was completely goal ori-ented. She believed in economy in everything, movement, speech, work, pain. Everything except laughter and happiness. In those areas no one would ever know she was a glutton. Only the people who were very close to her would understand that she would be the first one to get naked in the sunshine like a three year old and laugh like a hyena behind closed doors. She was a maniac, the boy child in the super chick body; and she loved to get life all over her. Penn had often busted her when he would leave for a meeting only to return to a hotel room to find her dancing on the bed to a video like a pre teen or dancing around naked with her Mp3 player shutting the world out enjoying being alone. Aria would be dancing and having a fabulous time, because she could. To her experience was to be alive.

Penn woke from his nap took a quick shower, dressed and went downstairs after a cell call from Mike. Mike and Frank were downstairs and they too were knawing their arms off from hunger. They went to a typical high end Middle Eastern restaurant in Karachi that Frank had cleared with Chamberlin and was patronized every once in a while. They walked into the restaurant and were thankful they were not the only Westerners in the room. Otherwise, it would have just been too uncomfortable. That was the one good thing about the higher end restaurants or hotel restaurants in parts of the Middle East. If the group was mixed then you didn't stick out being the only ant at the picnic. Thank God for small favors. The men sat down and enjoyed great local food. All three ate like it was their last meal, hummus and pita, babaghanoush and lamb and the food just kept coming. It was a euphoric feeling in a place where these three were usually very alone and not feeling so satisfied. Penn turned down his normal glass of red wine because of where they were and because of tomorrow's action packed agenda. Too bad it would have been nice to get a little buzz, but it would have been careless and amateurish and Penn was neither. They tried to be inconspicuous even quiet, but they were having a fantastic time and they attracted more than their share of attention. So… after a short period of time it was time to go.

They knew from experience that it was not safe to be any one place too long. This was not Kuwait or Dubai or even Jordan, so God help you if you let your guard down. The guys left and dropped Penn off and he made his way upstairs making sure he had no one tailing him. He checked his room before and after he entered. Penn washed up, set up the room for an intrusion and then he slipped into bed. He tried to read a book that some-one had given him but fell asleep with the book on his chest after about a page and a half. With all the reading he did for work and the amount of information he processed weekly it was understand-able. He just didn't have it in him at all to ingest any more mate-rial in his spare time… all fifteen minutes of it. Penn drifted off to sleep with thoughts of going home to his girls and Aria. There in Karachi he was grateful this first night that he was alive and going to sleep in a bed for a change with a full belly not too bad, not too bad at all.

CHAPTER NINETEEN

Morning came too quickly and he was up early. Penn packed his brief case and laid out his journalist attire on the bed. Penn had a couple of contacts reach through to set up two meetings by email and one followed up with a phone call. As he prepared, someone with whom he had never spoken reached out to him by phone to make sure the meeting was still on. Penn was informed by the voice that he would be getting another phone call this morning to make sure he was available, and yet another caller would tell him where to be and when. Operations like this always put people on edge especially in this part of the world. But much of this operation would be carried out at night which would make it even more creepy. With all the unpaved roads and the lack of infrastructure the landscape always looked like it had been bombed. Typical of the third world roads were generally rotten and dusty at best, if there was even a road at all. In neighborhoods there were mud packed walls around homes much as existed in the Middle Ages.

Some of the worst bedlam was around the Pirwadi bus station; it was always a mess and Penn did his best to stay away from the vicinity at all costs. Just getting around was always a task, a security issue and nothing short of a total pain in the ass. When countries are poor, most Americans have absolutely no idea of what peoples lives are like completing simple tasks. Everything takes so much time and effort, it's exhausting.

Penn made his calls to Mama Bear and put everything on course for his faithful trajectory. He checked on everything at Langley and then sat down to eat. Luckily he was still so full from last night that he only had a meager appetite. He had packed some cheese, pepperoni and crackers in a small leather duffel bag. His head always rested easier when he had more food rather than less to keep on his person in a foreign country, especially in Pakistan. Now the drill was to wait. Hurry up and wait. The first phone call came in shortly before 8: 30 a.m. The caller was checking to confirm the interview. Langley was on the phone the whole time. Clay had already been up for hours despite the nine hour time difference. He was waiting like Penn, like a moray eel in a cave. They had the newest Jihadie bullshit phone number and the info went straight from Penn's phone with Clay on the line and then he relayed to Penn's housecleaner's on the ground in Pakistan.

The first meeting was set for just after breakfast and then there would be even more waiting. The clean up team would be busy this evening. They could not clean up and operate too early or it would be all over town spread mouth to mouth, and Penn would not be able to get back in time. The bad guys would originally try to set the meeting for 10:30 am and Penn would say he was caught in another interview with someone. But everyone knew it was bullshit, because "the subject" would be working for us the whole time.

Penn would ask to reschedule the interview for later but he would not attempt to change the place. It would be preferable, there would be less people on the street as well and it would be easier to move about. The call came and they bought it. They let Penn move the time as long as he didn't try to move the place so they would still retain the control, the home court advantage. Penn left the hotel and proceeded to the first interview. The venue was a restaurant. Penn arranged for a private room. That made Penn's job easier since it's harder to kill or threaten someone in public. Penn arrived by cab and was led into the back room in the restaurant where he met a small group of people whom he thankfully had never ever seen before. Considering this was Karachi, that might keep him from being shot again. Good to know, note to self.

The interview commenced and things went as planned. Penn planted some bugs and managed to confirm all the identities at the meeting and met his objectives. To keep his image and cover clean however; he never completed the termination section of the show. Rather, he got to terminate and he knew the outcome; he just did not have to do all that sticky dirty stuff that makes it harder to move about the cabin, post haste. With the targets confirmed and the escape plan set, Penn got out of the meeting safely, though it got a little dicey.

He called in the "LFM" or better know as "Langley's Flying Monkeys" as Aria liked to call them. "The LFM" let Penn get to a safe place away and across town and let the bad guys feel safe and secure through the end of their day. Then, as Penn was back at the hotel planning the next interview and laying out the schedule with target number two for the evening, "The LFM" swooped in did the wet work and helped the small group of Jihadie crazies meet their beloved Allah–no plastic explosives or virgins included. Back at Langley if they didn't have another group for the "LFM" to visit that night, they would have thrown a party around the water cooler, but they were still working. They would be working for a while because they still had men and women on the ground. The only thing that would stop them would be 100% occupancy at a domestic US military base with an airplane load of people who would need a great deal of sleep and a bath and a sit down meal.

Penn called Clay again. They discussed the upcoming target and the different scenarios for him getting out of Pakistan, if things got a little squirrelly. And things got squirrelly a lot. Sometimes it happens, the shit hits the fan and if it's been planned for at least you aren't shocked and you can react and solve a big problem without thinking.

Clay and Penn wrapped up their call and Penn waited for the next call from another fixer. This time Penn knew the drill would be different. His fixer was not the person who called him, it was a new person. Penn thought it was the fixer for the fixer. "In Pakistan, there was a web of Jihadie bullshit that went with every situation." It took enormous patience to deal with all the crap knowing you could get into a tight spot at every turn. "They were such unbelievable cowards hiding behind all of their brain washed religious crap in everything. It was an unwritten cultural rule like the Nazi's in WWII. Most of the populous just condoned it and looked the other way."

For a moment Penn stood there in the window knowing better than to go out on the balcony, the sun set to the west, orange, red, purple and yellow. Penn thought of home and hoped that before he saw the sun again that he would be on a jet headed west headed for home. The phone rang in his hand, startling him momentarily, because for a minute he was lost in the sky. The creepy foreign voice on the other end of the phone told him to go over to a specific hotel and a told him that he would be notified about the room number. He packed the last of his gear and within 5 minutes he was in the elevator; which looked like it was built in Europe in the 1800 s. Penn was sure that somewhere in the basement there was a very tired donkey being led around a pole to raise and lower the elevator. He felt guilty every time he used it. He got over the images of the wretched donkey and the spectral sky and emerged from the hotel into the chaos of the street.

Thankfully it was getting late and people were struggling to get home for the evening, so the streets were getting easier to navigate. The time could not have been better. Penn was over it, less than 48 hours had expired and once again he was over Karachi. He could not imagine why... While walking away from the hotel to pick up a cab he got a call from Clay to let him know that the cleanup team had great success and that the first portion of the operation was complete. Penn was relieved to also hear the guys already were in place at his next destination. He finished the call with Clay before he hopped in the cab. He never liked to be in closed unsecured areas when receiving or making a call. Penn knew the consequences of being careless. He never liked to take chances. He found a cab he deemed safe and flagged the driver. He spoke some broken Urdu and told him to drive to a specific hotel across town.

It took about 10 minutes even this late in the day before the blood suckers of Karachi had re- emerged onto the streets for the evening. Putting on his game head en route by the time the cab stopped in front of the hotel, he was as ready as ready gets. He made his way in and strode across the lobby and to the elevator. He looked for any security people whom his advance team may not have noticed or that no one may have told him about. He paid attention to the layout and to alternative exits from the building. He got a room number by text as soon as he reached the lobby so he knew where he was going and he knew that someone was aware of his arrival. This was meant to be unnerving, and 602 was all it said. Penn had no idea what he would face when he got inside.

For all he knew the door could have been rigged with a plastic explosive. Who the hell knows, it could be anything. He got to floor six and was so pleased to see that there was no one in the hall and there did not appear to be a surveillance system. Penn knocked on the door while standing off to the side. Someone came to the door to open it. They asked him for ID in perfect English with the queen's accent, obviously someone went to school in London and they came from money. That was better than most here. These guys were not like most rookies or low level planners. The target was an accomplished asshole with a track record.

Penn entered the room and the door closed behind him. Those inside patted him down and took his briefcase for just a moment. When they were satisfied that they knew who they were dealing with they gave it back. Then they asked him to sit down and take out a pen and paper and take some notes. The three creepy guys and Penn had a chat. He was introduced to everyone and then when they felt secure one left the room to fetch some food. They figured the journalist was going to be there for awhile and so they had a captive audience to spew some of their rhetoric to the western journalistic machine. Once it became two on one, they never knew what hit them. With one Jihadie on a food run, and the other Jihadie preparing a car to change location. Before the third could even return with food Penn had dispatched the gentle persons and the clean up team was already moving into place. Some came through the front door of the hotel and some came through the window.

Penn slipped out into the hall, and got busted by a guy who he had seen on the way in. Not good and so the chase ensued. The best option was to get the hell out without getting caught. Penn hauled ass jumping out a third story window. With his fall broken by a small pile of sand that had just been abandoned by a undisciplined construction crew. He rolled in to a run and before he could catch his breath he was being chased at top speed down an alley by a group of Jihadie crazies as bullets rained down all around him while they yelled at him and each other in Urdu. Penn made a turn and dodged in to a smaller side street where he saw an old man with an ice cream cart with a skirt around it. He threw his body under the cart and prayed that the old man he encountered would not rat him out as the Jihadies got closer on their hunt for him. He wished the whole time that he had been wearing his running shoes but hey when it's your ass you make it work. The elderly man could have turned Penn over to the Jihadies as they were now swarming the area, but he didn't. When things calmed down a bit Penn called Clay and screamed at him about his cleanup team back at the hotel and about sending in the cavalry to rescue his ass ASAP. "Damn it Clay, where the fuck is my team?" "I need to get out of here now!" "What good is the damn GPS if nobody is picking me up?" Stay put Penn we're almost there, Clay answered calmly. It's been a shit storm all day Clay, I get it, but it's gonna cost ya, put me through... now. Penn dials Aria. "Hi Baby, what are you doing?"

"Oh busy one... my my. Wrong shoes today huh? You've been busy, how are you now?" "It's been a little stupid but it's improving." "Good can you call me when everything is stable in a little while?" "Sure Baby, I'll let you know." "I love you Penn." "I love you too sweet- heart, gotta go my rides here, I'll call, bye." Up charged a large black Escalade which screeched to a halt and the door closest to Penn flew open at the end of the small street that he ran down. It was too narrow for the large vehicle to get any-where near the little old man's ice cream cart that Penn was using as a fort.

When the team showed up to retrieve him they had both been on the phone with Clay and his team almost the entire time. Penn sprinted for the vehicle, he was then taken to a safe place to wait until his unique and exceedingly private transportation situation could be arranged out of the country. No one on this team under these circumstances could say enough about private aviation. It was a beautiful thing and Penn was about to experience the most exclusive baggage recovery service on the planet. There was no going back to the room to retrieve his baggage and personal effects, so someone was sent immediately. They packed his gear, tore the room apart made it look like a robbery and got it out of there. His bags would then meet him wherever they decided to take or send him. No one knew where the second jumping off point would be yet. If it wasn't someplace in Europe it would be someplace back on terra firma USA. Everything would be perfect. In this situation this was what you called a job perk. The ultimate in removal and relocation.

Penn also was regularly in a position where he ended up los-ing things, or being re routed or having no clothes in a foreign land during an operation. So when these little problems reared their nasty heads things would just show up. Penn would be some-where and all the sudden he would get a gift bag like a Hollywood Oscar party without the face cream and the expensive shampoo. Here's your custom sized tux, shoes and all your clothes and toi-letries and they are in a new carry on case. It was definitely one of the better perks of the job, but considering the tradeoffs, which could be bloody, it was really the least that the group could do for their top dogs. Penn waited in the safe place with a small team and then everything was in online courtesy of Clay and his team back at the home office. Everyone had been walking on eggshells and the local team was anxious to deliver Penn to his next group of handlers. It wasn't always so glamorous. In fact most of the time it wasn't. It just worked out that sometimes it got crazy hot very fast and it worked out with the other big dogs able to get in low under the radar and assist. Many times Penn had to get his own ass out. In fact, those contingencies were always discussed and planned just in case, because you absolutely never knew how it was going to go. It wasn't even possible to tell once you got on the ground. Things were so fluid, all the time that you just had to wait and look around and see what was going to happen. Clay always tried to discuss and plan for as many contingencies as possible, he was always good like that. Not plan A and B, but plan A through F.

The team waited until late in the evening and then put Penn in a car in a hidden compartment in the back. Clay had told Penn and his locals that it was now time to get out and that there would be a helo waiting for him at certain coordinates and that it would fly him safely over the boarder into India where he would be picked up. Clay had quickly cleared everything with the Indians and found the chopper and the bilingual pilot capable of flying with no lights in the darkest night. Clay had helped save the day or at least the second half of it. Clay would monitor the whole operation from the sky in real time and know exactly what was happening every minute. The pilot would be foreign, but he would be flying American hardware for an American institution. He would fly Penn to a safe place. All of Penn's fears were quashed by Clay before he got a chance to think. He just wanted to get the hell out. Like Penn, Clay and everyone else on the team was cracker jack. Clay knew he would not breathe until Penn touched down in India. Then it would be a full team sigh not relaxation yet... but a sigh.

Once again they would fly low under the radar and it would be dicey; Al Qaeda and their sympathizers loved their shoulder fired rocket launchers. And they had plenty of them and knew how to use them which was a constant source of angst for all the good guys. Looking for buried weapons was like a daily Easter egg hunt. It was only great when you found some, otherwise it was always dangerous and it made every day suck.

The local team got Penn out to the coordinates issued by Clay's office and that was the flight line in the middle of nowhere. The trip out while relatively short seemed to take forever. "No matter how well prepared everyone was everybody was extremely anxious under these operational conditions." Time went by and they were driving without lights so thank God the moon was high that night. They started to get close to the pre determined coordinates, so they needed to slow down and watch the sky to the east. They pulled off the road, cutting the engine when they hit the mark. The agent riding shotgun pulled out tiny night vision binoculars and scanned the sky to the east and the south. He watched the American issue unmarked military chopper fly over the brown mountainous desert like a shadow in the night, out of nowhere. Like a vampire bat, efficient almost stealth like aerodynamic, quiet and faster than you would expect. Penn couldn't help but think that it reminded him of the national symbol even in the dark. Like a huge eagle proud and strong and with big wings and ultimate control over itself not giving a damn, and always working to be on the side of right.

Penn was proud to be a part of operations like this, especially when things went so well. Even though Penn's activities were often blacker than black, he liked to be a good guy. Everyone always understood that some data points were better left unknown and unsaid. This was one of those times.

It was a bit naive and insane to think that most Americans, everyday people could process or handle all this violent craziness, and contrary to popular belief the world is a brutal nasty place. All the field operatives were trained and designed to deal with and process all the stress. Penn felt good about protecting people and he always tried to do the moral and correct thing; for the most part so did everyone else. After what seemed like an eternity the chopper got close, and the pilot and the ground crew both had visual and acknowledged. Langley patched the pilot through to the guys on the ground and he hovered before setting down. At the last minute Penn jumped out of the vehicle and ran for the chopper with Clay in his and everyone else's ear.

The door to the chopper flew open and Penn took the shot-gun seat. He buckled in and put on his headgear and helmet and waved to the men that helped save his life. Even if he never saw them again he would never forget the three or four hours that they spent watching over him. He figured out that one way or another he would run into these agents again... probably in Pakistan. Penn would have been good if Pakistan got put on his list of no go places but he was more experienced than that and he knew that he would be back again, it was just a matter of time.

They lifted off quietly, almost silently, and headed east and a little south. It would be hours before the sun got up. Penn took a moment and looked back at the ground at where they just came from. He watched the agents fade away into a dot in the distance. He thought about standing in the window back at the hotel, and then his thoughts wandered to the part of the day when he got to the to dispatch the bad guys. He took his first breath and had a hard time not letting the sound of the rotor and the rocking of the helo put him to sleep like so many types of transportation did. Before long they would cross the border. He felt blessed to be with such a safe and highly capable pilot. The guy was Indian and Penn thought Clay really knew his shit. The pilot had introduced him-self as Rupee and everyone on the line got a laugh. Penn would never have an issue with Clay's ability to run him again, he was in.

So while Clay was on the line and so was everyone else as they landed in India, Penn thanked Clay and the team on air. "Gen-tlemen" said Penn "I want to take this time to say thank you to everyone on air and everyone who put all of this online, Thank you Clay." Penn asked for a quiet line and Clay knew to block the Indian pilot's access to the line momentarily. He said to Clay "May I go ahead sir?" "Penn you are secure" Clay replied. "Now how did we do with clean up?" Clay replied "nothing but net buddy. It is a beautiful day thanks to you." "Fantastic, that makes me happy I know this was very important to you and to everyone else I am proud to have been a part of it. Thank you for the opportunity and for believing in me enough to let me try."

"Thank you Penn, it was everyone's pleasure. You righted a wrong today. You're having a career defining moment enjoy it, you deserve it. Now let me switch on the line again and speak to Rupee. Are we good?" "Yes, Clay we're good." "Hi Rupee, this is Clay at Langley, again. You're within range are you comfortable landing at set coordinates?" Rupee replied, "Yes sir, Roger that, I'm fine with it, and conditions are favorable." "Anything that I should know about?" "No, Rupee everything's online. Our team will be at set coordinates to pick up agent Penn. Thank you so much for your service, you really bailed our happy butts out on this one." "Please thank the Colonel again for me and regards to your wife for me, we'll see you in a few weeks okay."

"Okay, thanks Clay Sir, we will see you soon." "Agent Penn when we get down I'm going to shut her down, please wait for the blades to stop before getting out." "Fine. Thank you Rupee. It's been a pleasure." "Hope we get to fly together again under more optimum circumstances." "Yes, me too."

We see the team pull up in a large black bullet proof diplomatic, tinted window Escalade and a few agents get out to retrieve Penn from the helo. We see the blades slow to a stop, Penn shakes Rupee's hand and hands over his headgear and helmet. He opens the door and waves as he walked away. He turns towards the Escalade and finally takes a full breath for the first time in 36 hours. He was greeted by all three of the field agents.

The moment he climbed into the back seat he was handed protein bars and water by the top dog who sat with him while one of the other two agents drove and the third rode shotgun. Penn sank back into his seat. The sun was starting to come up and Penn reached for his sunglasses. He was not ready to see daylight yet since he had not slept. He felt like a vampire and knew that it would be a different world for him after he managed to get some rest. They were headed for a secure diplomatic location to allow Penn to shower, eat and get a couple hours of sleep after which they put him on a flight to Dulles Airport in Washington D.C. It had been another day and he was still here. Remarkable, he knew

Aria had been waiting so Penn shot her a text as soon as he got on the ground in India. Several hours later, Penn boarded an airplane and was never so happy to eat boring commercial airline food. He fell asleep sitting up somewhere over Eastern Europe and by the time they landed in France to refuel he barely woke. Uncharacteristically, he slept almost the whole way home to Washington.

He called Aria the minute he got his seat on the airplane. He told her that he loved her for the very first time. Then the cabin door had to be closed and he had to hang up. But Aria blurted out the perfect reply which made him a sleepy and happy man. There in the sky somewhere over India, Penn felt loved and knew that he was truly blessed in every way that someone can be. When they landed in Washington he almost felt human.

CHAPTER TWENTY

Penn and Aria had made a jump. A big jump. They knew that they would not get to spend Thanksgiving or Christmas together despite the sacrifices and the time that they had spent apart. They wanted to be together. They both felt obligated to be with their respective families, but they also were after something else–before the holiday they would meet in NYC. Aria's best case scenario. They would stay right off Times Square in a boutique hotel that was very hip and hidden and they both loved it. Another hideaway like their cave in Washington. Once again Aria was the recruiter for the newest nest and she found the perfect spot. She walked around NYC remembering how much she missed the city. As a child that was where she grew up and she was always comfortable there. Aria and Penn went to fabulous restaurants and places that no one would have expected to find them always flying low under the radar. It always calmed Aria down when she was put in a position to worry less. The business of saving the world kept their heads so preoccupied that sweet relief was any moment or hour when the burden could be lifted even a little bit.

About the only high profile activity they participated in during those days was to go see the tree at Rockefeller Center. Aria actually went two more times on her own without Penn, she missed it that much. Aria's family history in NYC was actually quite substantial and she had yet to deal with it emotionally. Aria never told Penn about her family's history in the city. She never told anyone or claimed it, until now.

They sat around and talked alot, in the bedroom and in restaurants and while having tea in the afternoon. They talked while taking walks on the street and in the park. From the very beginning they were gentle with each other. They made it a priority to be kind and to never yell at each other. Penn and Aria were each other's safe harbor. They lived in such a stress filled world, but the days in New York were full of intimate, poignant longing interjected with discussions on national security and politics. The amount of targeted communication and the intellectual activity was unmatched in any other relationship either one of them had ever experienced. But they could just as easily spoken about really risqué sex or physics and aerodynamics or medicine or national security all in the same breath.

Since time was their greatest friend and enemy they never squandered it. They treated it like a piece of fragile hand blown glass in a precious box. They guarded it with their lives. In fact these were presents that Penn would give her when they met. First a piece which reminded him of his mother and his grandmother, and then an ornament hand blown in Egypt. It was a ritual that Aria started with her gifts to Penn. Gifts of unique things. One of a kind things, that could not and would not be duplicated just like each of them. Unique in the world, precious by virtue of it's existence. Aria would make Penn things by hand, sometimes she would buy him great art.

In Aria's eyes Penn should always be surrounded by beautiful things, so she did her best to make that happen. The behavior bled over into everything they did, their laughter was the kind that makes you run to the bathroom while your eyes tear. The protective nature that they displayed was the filter that everything else was passed through. They would be goofy and insensitive together with no fear, speaking with accents or like they were stoned. There was no malice intended. They did it all in the name of play and maintaining their sanity; they screwed around constantly. They made terribly politically incorrect jokes and made fun of everyone, every single group starting with themselves. They did things together and in front of each other that they wouldn't dream of doing in front of anyone else. A testament to the level of trust and intimacy in the relationship. People in Washington and in politics would have been mortified. And in-between all of the childlike goofy behavior, they discussed, prepared and planned things that they could do in order to help steer everything that was good for the country. The days in New York were amazing, Penn and Aria moved about the city together quietly and snuggled in bed like puppies in heat.

CHAPTER TWENTY-ONE

I t was getting cold and grey in New York by now and even though there were many more things that they needed to do to learn about each other, they would have to wait. The trip ended far too soon and they had to go home for Thanksgiving. Penn had to go back into training in order to deal with the most specialized assignment that he had ever been offered. Quite frankly, nothing on earth compared, ever. Aria was not happy and knew what was coming and she was measuring every single breath because he once again would be in a unique situation that no one could ever know about. They would be separated during the holidays with Penn away over Christmas and New Years. He would be in such an unbelievably hostile and uniquely dangerous environment that it was almost unreal. And as usual, he would be out there all alone. He took the assignment, of course, because he was the only person that the agency felt was capable of handling it and they trusted him to be successful at all of it.

The set up and the training for the whole operation would rise to a level that the agency had never undertaken before... no one believed that they had ever encountered this specific a problem and task to tackle. Penn was now developing the mo of being the company guinea pig. Just the physical coordination for all the pieces to fall the way they had to be in order to get him placed in the position to carry out the mission was absurd.

Then to even get him the shot at pulling off the operation was formidable and that did not even take into account the operation itself. The caveat was the whole issue of completing the mission correctly and covering his tracks and escaping within the proper window to avoid being tracked. Which was an entirely different matter. The whole operation would be very dangerous with a high risk of him being killed. This operation was referred to as "going in and out of this den of vipers" by the operatives for high stakes and ultra dangerous missions that they got saddled with regularly.

For those who never had to do it, this transit was always made to sound a hell of a lot easier and substantially less complicated than it actually was. The comments during prep with some well meaning Mensa candidate always reflected this. Many of these people were not field guys so they did not truly grasp the nuances that only the guys on the ground understood from the bottom up. It's not trivial when it's your ass. For Penn, the trickiest part was covering the time away from his day job, making the excuses and building the illusion for everyone in his life to buy it all, hook line and sinker. The day came for Penn once again to head for points unknown and neither Penn nor Aria were looking forward to it. As usual, Aria was on the beach, waiting for Penn to hurry up and leave so he could return... quite literally in one piece. She tried to carry on her normal business and personal life while she counted the days, nights and sometimes the moments until they got to communicate in one form or another.

Until then she pretended, just like Penn, that things were normal. Aria never let on that she knew anything about issues of national security at the highest levels. She play acted that she was the same as the people that she encountered. That she was just a normal person and not an asset to the asset. She was less than a hairs breadth away from being a full fledged spy herself. It was an insanely uncomfortable position, with no support and on a weekly basis Aria's world went from worse to the kind of stress that makes people look for a very tall building or bridge that looks like a viable option.

She would listen to people while they complained about their mostly shallow, vapid, naïve, insipid lives–all the time thinking about all the agents in the field and the dangers they faced daily. She tried to not get irritated with people when they would be so selfish and short sighted. But there were times when all that she wanted to do was scream or ring their necks. Most of the time she could control herself. Occasionally, she would pop off and tip her hand, after which some poor, misinformed, ignorant soul would be left standing there with their brain in their hand, quivering from too much information. Aria, like Penn would often flash back in situations like that to when she and Penn were together or when she was alone which was most of the time. One time they were in the New York metropolitan area and they were hiding in a little hotel by a major university in a place where no one would ever know to look for people like them. Hiding in plain sight.

The weather was freezing with sheets of rain coming down sideways. Penn pulled up alongside of the hotel to be a gentleman and let Aria off at the door. She begged him not to do that and told him it would turn out badly. She was adamant and almost in tears. He got a little upset and told her to get out of the car. She did what he asked, though begrudgingly. Aria, of course, was correct and by the time Penn got back from the car to where she was standing, there was a group of rednecks that had engaged and Aria was ready to put her foot through a gentleman's skull in order to protect herself. Up to that point, Aria wondered what the hell was taking Penn so long and was hoping that he would hurry up so she wouldn't have to do what she knew she was going to have to do which would have gotten very messy quickly. She wasn't interested in having Penn be her clean up crew with the cops and spending the night in the police station, instead of in bed making love. Penn arrived in the nick of time and his formidable size put an interesting twist on the whole situation. He put two and two together the second he arrived; he was happy that she had run out into the rain to meet him. When he looked at her and saw her there vibrating in the rain, he couldn't yell. She was like a lightening bolt in the rain.

glowing on a charger. She never said a word, she never had to. He knew she wouldn't be standing there if she didn't need to be. He walked towards the building with her. He was happy that she had come out to meet him and did not take the guy's head off. He knew better than to be around if anyone threatened his girl because that would be a like threatening him, and that would be a very bad move.

Penn understood about Aria now. That you do not threaten someone who has been under it because, male or female, they will do what they have to much faster than average and size has nothing to do with the final outcome. Penn now realized that Aria had tried to warn him. Needless to say that from then on, Penn never questioned the tiny girl again. When she balked, he always listened. He knew she never shot her mouth off. Every time she warned him about something, as far as she was concerned, her credibility was on the line. So she never was cavalier. Her only interest was to protect people. She never did it for her own benefit. After a while Penn knew that her "abilities and instincts", as he called them, were more accurate than any instrument. He had never seen and he had never experienced anything quite like it. He always called when she "wanted" him to, everyone did. She just held the phone in her hand and it would ring nearly every single time.

The run up to the intensity of this whole Christmas fiasco had left both of them feeling terribly guilty and frustrated. They wanted to have a place together. They wanted to be someplace different with their own tree and have a blended family. They weren't even to the point of buying presents for each other for the holidays, but they were just lying to themselves as they were way past that emotionally. Penn had to make one more trip to a facility before going out on assignment, which made Aria happy. She knew where he was and she knew he was safe and fed. Aria loved that peace of mind. She loved the benefit of not having to tear her heart out for days and weeks with worry. Penn was taken care of when he was "under the wing" for a short period of time and it calmed her. He was unique and she trusted that his handlers would guard their investment. She also knew that they wanted to clone him. She was quite sure that the company would have been very pleased if they decided to have some children and then share the superhero genetics. That would have been their best case scenario, cloning, no Petri dish necessary. But Penn and Aria knew that they would never get to do the family thing, so they guarded their hearts. So in light of that fact and it being the holidays they committed to staying busy until the time when they could finally be exactly where they wanted to be. They were literally waiting to let their lives catch up to where their hearts and minds had already started living as one.

On that last trip to New York, Aria gave Penn a small token of her affection so he would understand that she was already working hard with him to build traditions of their own. Aria had purchased a Christmas ornament that she found in her favorite store.

When Aria saw it in the store, she had to own it and give it to Penn. It sparkled like a diamond. Somehow it felt beautiful and precious and mushy. Aria was completely obsessed with giving it to him to put on his Christmas tree, in hopes that the following year or the year after that it would end up on a very different Christmas tree, one that they could call their own. A Christmas tree placed somewhere in a house called their first. First house and Christmas tree, first Christmas preceded by a whole year of collecting Christmas ornaments for the tree. These were the simple little things that she dreamed of daily, for the very first time in her life. The stakes got higher physically and emotionally, for both of them every time he went out. As their lives became more intertwined and they needed each other more, they eventually reached a point where neither one could picture their lives without the other in it. Their relationship became very intense, and for the first time, both of these lone wolves who never needed anyone, looked at being joined to someone at the hip as a truly viable option. To Penn and Aria, marriage meant death. Aria had felt like this long before these days came to pass, based entirely on her marriage and divorce a few years before, which basically equated to skydiving with no parachute. It was so abusive, that jumping from a plane for survival felt like a better option and done completely for self preservation. Admittedly, marriage still scared her beyond reproach.

There was almost nothing that scared her more. When referring to the possibility of marriage she would say... "Give me the gun" and then she would gesture. For Penn he couldn't remember when he was not married, he had always been married. And he also never wanted to get married again, when hell froze over maybe. Lately though, according to Penn and Aria, you could ski in hell.

Penn had been so unhappy having made such a huge mistake and having stayed that way decades past his "use by" date. Marriage was not even on his radar. Then he met Aria, and the whole idea just flew out the window like the mistake never even existed. Until then Penn and Aria both had a total and complete aversion to "the M word" or "the dirty word" as Aria referred to it. It was too strong a concept for either one of them. But Penn got there emotionally first, in fact months before Aria and even though they were both scared of what it might bring they both admitted the fact that they thought that it was some place that maybe they should be. And even that was a side step and a denial of the idea as a whole. Marriage, just the thought of the word, made Aria throw up in her mouth just a little bit. It upset every bodily function it gave her gas and nausea. She did not know what to do. She oscillated between almost not being able to deal with the concept; to being "all in" and thinking it was the sexiest idea on the planet and that should have happened already. Aria was not used to being so schizophrenic about anything.

The girl who never had problems with making any kind of decision, about anything regardless of the circumstances, was completely perplexed about the idea of marriage. Something that most of the human race made terrible decisions on or viewed as the next logical step or as a way to have children or empowerment, money, status, a regular sex partner, companionship, a visa, an identity, a change of citizenship. Seems few married for what Aria thought were good reasons, and Aria did not view marriage as a reason to further most of the causes. Especially the possibility of marrying an agent and the pressure of becoming one yourself.

She was factoring in all the insanity, time apart, the worry, the pain, and of course the ever present possibility of Penn coming home in a hefty bag, and her heart being broken beyond repair for all of eternity. But she was willing to entertain the idea because she loved him so and she could never see her way clear to loving anyone else or being loved in the same way by anyone else on the planet. She had already seen too much to believe that someone else could love her like he did.

Then there was the safety–the way she felt because he was in the world in the first place. From the first moment she met him, she knew he was protecting her. Aria was used to doing all the protecting. The only person who had ever been capable of making her feel this way was her father. Now that this Freudian faux paux was sitting on her chest and she had to deal with him.

The part that actually made Aria relinquish control long enough to let someone else make her feel safe that was the yummiest part of all. He was capable and not only did she feel safe when she was with him, she actually was safe. He continued to prove this time and again and it really revved Aria's engines, but she never let on or he would have done it all the time. Every time Penn did something correctly she responded like Pavlov's dog and had to fight the urge to bite him and drag him to bed wherever they were. It was just so primal, she felt like she was always on the hunt for a broom closet. Miss Manners meets the broom closet. It was a constant merry war betwixt sex in safety and privacy, and crazy, primal passion.

CHAPTER TWENTY-TWO

P enn flew from New York to Canada, he had a layover, a change of venue, and then he disappeared off the face of the planet, as if he was smoke. Once again he was blacker than black. Most people who thought they knew what was actually going on, didn't. Leaks were a constant threat and Penn always guarded against them. So called stories that supposedly were shared with a Hollywood producer who then makes a movie more often than not, is crap. Anyone who really has access to the real deal knew it. The crap that they rant about on the news; this person is so bad and that guy did such and such … the vanity that leads everyone to think that the press, the general public and 99% of Capitol Hill could handle it or keep their collective pie hole shuts, is absurd.

There are certain kinds of deeds that must be done to keep everyone alive. They never get written down in any form, ever. There are no records! Put on your big boy underroos and deal with it. But Aria knew where Penn was and what was going down and where he was headed next. He never told her yet she managed to figure it out as he traversed every step across one continent after another all the way to his destination. Further along he made a jump to the place "where Ringo met a girl" and Aria had her mind's eye confirmed from a comment in cyberspace. Aria and Penn knew better for security purposes than to get specific in their voice and text messages. There was always some vague notion about the weather or some ridiculous joke completely unrelated to any of the operational directives.

At first Penn did not understand that he never needed to go into lengthy explanations. Aria would say to Penn, "I've got it Baby." She was always afraid some bad guy would overhear them either by eavesdropping electronically or by someone being in close proximity. For the longest time Penn never believed her but that was before he knew. She picked up on all the details spoken and unspoken, even the ones referencing times when she had not yet been born. After a whole day and many verbal and virtual hugs and kisses and bytes, he arrived via a special team that he had flown with a couple of times before under similarly volatile conditions. This was the best team on the planet for this specific type "extreme flying"; the kind that no one else had the experience or the balls to tackle. Despite the captain and crew's amazing abilities, you would think that Penn would be reticent to fly again, but he wasn't. One of the times Penn had flown with one of the team's pilots, he had pulled a "Full Sully" and crash landed under very harsh conditions. A lesser pilot and crew would have screwed the pooch. Obviously they lived to tell the tale, but now they had a bigger problem, survival in a subzero environment with gale force winds. Their operation and the geography were highly classified, as in it did not exist. There was no rescue party on speed dial. Penn was the only one who had brought along food and water. Several days elapsed before they were found, and it was Penn who provided the sustenance. His preparation and quick thinking were the thing that almost always saved the day.

Aria told Penn months ago that the wives knew nothing about their husbands real lives and that all the gentlemen were immensely grateful to Penn because of his actions years before when they crashed for the first time... it happens. They were all grateful as well to the pilot who had made it possible for everyone on that plane to experience many more hugs, Christmases and sunsets, grandkids and weddings, smiles and family times through the years. It humbled Penn and made him proud at the same time. He was happy to be a part of something bigger than himself, bigger than the time he was allotted.

He was known for being level. If Penn could control it, he could probably make it work one way or another. More often than not, it was "another," because that was pretty much his daily job description. Make it work, whatever it took. This particular saga was like a real life bad adventure movie so it wasn't like Penn had a hard time flying with these cats again. If there was any group that was set up to fly under the world's harshest conditions it was this specific group of gentlemen. The minute Penn hit the flight line, it was like old home week for hardcore survivors. The cold and the night and the black of this operation could not have chilled the warmth that could have roasted marshmallows that night, these people were family. They knew each other, intimately. They had all spent real character building time together over the years. On many occasions thinking that it was "game over" multiple times, but they pulled through together. They all had a great deal of respect for each other's specific abilities and personality traits as well as love for each other as individuals. None of these guys would ever leave a man behind.

They all buckled in for a long, multi-stop, challenging ride to a thankless, inhospitable environment. It would be the best part of the year to fly into the region, but to say it would be anything short of terrifying getting in or out, would be delusional. In point of fact, it would be a nightmare. By necessity these guys all had cast iron stomachs or they could not have done 99% of the work they performed weekly. They made the hurricane and tornado pilots look like cutesy little girls flying model airplanes. For starters, the hours these guys kept were insane and when they worked, they almost never slept. The limits to which they regularly pushed their equipment and their bodies to under extreme conditions was almost comical. A normal day at the office for them was filled with the promise of major bloodletting. Penn was strapped in and bumping around in the thin frigid air as they refueled and readied their rituals before they left the last semblance of civilization as the aircraft headed due south.

Before they took off however, Penn called Aria from the flight line and thought about what any of their wives or kids knew about what these gentlemen surrounding him did for a living. The answer was nothing... the people who loved all of these men had absolutely no clue what they really did for a living except Aria. As for the rest of the group they believed their Daddy or their spouse was a pilot. They also believed a variation on a theme about Daddy being gone a few days and then he would come back with a tan or an ice burn which was really a compression wound or shrapnel spray.

Then he would share some bullshit story about being in Costa Rica or on a corporate jet job and falling while surfing. These were the stories that got shared with co workers or by 6 year olds at show 'n tell, when they got asked by the teacher what their families jobs were. Many of the little kids believed their Dad's actually were superheroes, after all they flew airplanes for their job! From the mouths of babes, amazing that no one knew what superheroes they were calling "daddy or sweetheart" over the morning Cheerios. After what seemed like days of no sleep and a lot of shake rattle and roll, the team neared their destination. Tim, the pilot landed the bird on the biggest white blanket of ice and snow you could imagine. To Penn it felt like the surface of the moon. It was one of the scariest, sprawling, most desolate and unforgiving, places on the planet. Here people really needed each other. Without the trappings of human existence, death would be swift, quiet and ugly, unless you happened to be a polar bears next meal.

The fatigue from feeling like you had ridden the bull at Gilley's for five consecutive days on no sleep probably compared to how everyone felt when they stepped off the aircraft and into the frigid air. It was so cold that any exposed skin would freeze almost immediately. They had been advised to cover up as they made their way to an all terrain vehicle for a short trip to base camp to find food and their quarters to sleep.

The party that met them on the flight line was a curious mix of multilingual scientists from around the world as well as the project coordinator. The people there to greet them was by far was the weirdest group of frigid lab rats ever, Penn thought. He had observed from the get go how wide eyed and hollowed out these folks were. This base and all science projects had firm rules about how long scientists were allowed to remain out on any assignment. There was good reason for this; the base commander had the task of weeding out "The Willies" as people came to be known. "The Willies", slowly and sometimes quickly, spiraled into primal animal behaviors and madness. People had a tendency to lose their minds here and it did not take much to push some over the edge. It happened with a great degree of regularity in fact. It creeped Penn out. Aria warned Penn about such dangers specifically in advance. She used the "Children of the Corn" reference and even though that was not her frame of reference... it worked, but a better reference for him would have been "Deliverance".

The science stations population consisted of highly intelligent, under-stimulated people, albeit in a remote hostile environment. Penn just happened to be the fresh meat of the day, "it" the journalist of the season. To some souls their "it" was a culinary offering.

Really smart people with negative intent can do so much more damage than people of lesser intelligence. There really is no contest. Penn would take stupid people on a mission all day long, it's no big deal. "However, someone who is bored with malice and hyper intelligence is comparatively Hannibal Lector, and that is scary in a closed and isolated environment like this." At camp, the team was greeted warmly. They were quickly fed and assigned bunks and encouraged to get some sleep. It was not a moment too soon, since as everyone was almost too tired to stand. Which made the surreal surroundings and extreme cold even more offensive and foreboding. Cold, hungry and tired, the big three get even the most formidable animals attention.

Being cooped up in that plane did a number on everyone's judgment. Life seemed like a moving, morphing Dali painting bizarre, slightly grotesque, yet mesmerizing. Penn needed to get rest because tomorrow it would be game on, and he had a mission to complete. The rest of the team would get to leave tomorrow, weather permitting. Penn was so envious that they had the orders to leave, that he could have spit. But if he did it would have frozen anyway. He slept like a dead man and much to his dismay got up when he needed to; his body was so conditioned that it was frightening.

Uniquely, today he loathed getting up because he was finally warm, he rolled out of his bunk. He managed an uplink and went to the main dining room and was surprised beyond belief. There was photographic evidence strewn about, on desks and in work stations, and on bulletin boards. These mental giants partied like it was the end of the world whenever they got the chance. They were full fledged party animals, go figure. The suffering for the environment that was innate here was countered by the internal environment that had been created to distract people. Fabulous food and all sorts of extra curriculars, any movie you could think of, a great library, pool tables, you name it. Everyone's personal space was cluttered up with personal trinkets and knick knacks. Penn was amazed at the humanity of it all in the middle of nowhere, or more precisely at the end of nowhere. He walked around exploring before his scheduled meeting with the site director whom he had met last night. He learned a great deal just by saying "hello" to the people he encountered. Penn only had a rough idea of how many people were on site, so that would be a question for the upcoming meeting in about an hour.

After tooling around the vast complex and investigating a few wings he got the lay of the land, so he wandered back to the mess hall and found his breakfast. He managed to find turkey sausage, eggs and cereal and wash it down with some orange juice. He was famished because of all the flying under terrible conditions was not conducive to food consumption. He had not eaten well since the first flight more than 36 hours ago. He helped himself to seconds and still managed to get to the director's office on time despite getting lost...twice. The place was huge and maze like and besides he was jet lagged. All the hallways looked the same, much like a huge ship.

In one of the hallways he bumped into Tim the pilot and some of the team. They were going out later because the weather was on their side. The team was slept and getting in line to be fed, and feeling full of piss and vinegar again. They were anxious to get underway. Penn wanted to go too but like one of Snow White's Seven Dwarfs, Penn uttered, "Hi ho hi ho it's off to work I go." Everyone laughed and Penn hustled off to his meeting. He told the guys he would see them in about ten days if nice weather held out. Of course Capt. Tim echoed back "10 days" and they went their separate ways. "Be safe" Tim said to Penn, looking back over his shoulder. Penn nodded and the two had a moment. "You too," Penn said. Both had big jobs ahead of them and yet neither was supposed to know the true nature of the other's mission.

Aria was calm for the moment knowing that Penn had just arrived and had slept and eaten. She knew that he was safe at least for a spell before things would start to get weird on the third day. Once again, she was ahead of the curve. Even though he had rested, she worried about his ability to think clearly when things started to get dicey in a few days. Things would get aggressive and up in your face. Then Penn would not be safe and he would be trapped. There would be nowhere to run or hide, nowhere to retreat to if things got really hot. Leaving the compound for any length of time meant death, plain and simple.

You could not be outside, period. You could not wander from the compound. Weather and white out conditions were daily occurrences, even at the most benign time of year. When Aria got information that was specific about a situation, she would be water hosed and there could be too much information in her head to process all at the same time. She would give Penn the information about what she knew in the same way. He always wrote things down when he spoke to her on the phone, so he could refer to the specific warnings that she gave him. Aria was actually trying to sleep this first day of Penn's field trip, knowing her peace of mind and his safety would not last.

CHAPTER TWENTY-THREE

The first real day was proving to be quite productive and the meeting with the director went well, and Penn got his interview. The director took Penn on a more exclusive tour of the facility. He filled Penn up with all sorts of facts about this unique scientific experiment / station and its inhabitants. They spoke about the challenges of being basically the mayor of what amounted to a small town, micro-society on the tundra; point in fact... in the tundra as most of this facility was built well into and under the ground. He let Penn know that there was a specific rule about fraternizing between men and women because it bred so many complications to daily life. Babies, whether you like them or not would be the least of the complications that would come from people having sex. In fact, to counter peoples natural instincts, there was a porn room to keep the gentlemen in the facility at least semi level, and some women used it too. There was every type of porn imaginable and a specific place to take care of business. The gentlemen were encouraged to use this room often and liberally. Penn took a pass on the option while he was a visitor. But he made sure to tell Aria all about the room because he found the concept fascinating. He felt like he was hanging out in a combination jack shack and infertility clinic or a sperm bank. It was seedy and clinical at the same time. Their wasn't a damn thing sexy about it, it was like a bad job.

Later that night he saw the hints of the seedy underground that was alive and well as any place on the planet where human beings were concentrated. Indeed, where there were people, there would be sex. Male and female sex, gay sex, bestiality, sex with vegetables, whatever. If you could conjure it up, there was someone, somewhere doing it. Apparently, there were scads of people there and the vast majority were all doing it, pretty much constantly. Penn kept some strange hours and because of his job, he learned all about the weirdness of the entire enclave day after day. But it never got dark and the whole facility worked on a 24 hour time schedule, there were shifts. It stopped down, it just never slept. Just like New York or Vegas or Beijing. The proverbial 24 hour ant colony in the snow. All snow all daylight, all the time. Penn would wake in the "middle of the night" and bust three different people sneaking back to their quarters from someone else's, doing the "walk of shame" when they got busted by the newbie.

Turns out that the facility doctor was the town carnival ride, he was sleeping with more people than anyone. He promised with his Hippocratic Oath to care for everyone and apparently he really meant it! The whole facility was a "Clue" board game with a serious porn element.

Other than the fact that it would get wildly dangerous, Penn thought that the twisted nature of the whole hostile situation was quite amusing at a visceral level. It was real and completely unreal all at the same time. A total contradiction. Just like outside of the facility, eerily beautiful and serene, while being completely dangerous and lethal all in the same breath.

Aria took care to warn Penn about the aggressive chicks and the weirdo guys, not just the foreign operatives that would be targeting him. Also the scary guys that would try to ID him and thwart his mission. If they managed to find him, they would surely try to bring the journalist's world to a quick and painful end. Penn knew between scoping out the place in his prep and what he had to do and that it would be pretty standard. This was his job, wherever he did his interviews, it always seemed like standard operating procedure. But based on Penn's job description there was nothing normal about any of Penn's days. The director set up all of Penn's meetings with the key players in each of the departments. Thankfully, he cut Penn's learning curve and saved him a great deal of time. Most of the department heads were pretty accommodating and some could even be considered nice. Others were downright weird and / or spooky. By the third day, Penn had done quite a bit of checking and snooping around. He was looking to ID all of the necessary players in each program. His progress was swift and someone in one of the programs came up with the idea that the journalist be given something to really write about, he wanted to show Penn some offsite areas for study.

Of course, Penn had to pretend to be amazingly positive about the prospect of an offsite field trip with a half a dozen weird total strangers in the middle of nowhere. Needless to say he was not pleased, but he needed to go along and make it look good. The drill when a field trip ensued was that the director gave someone in the group a high powered rifle, because there was the ever present problem of free range polar bears that liked to feast on humans who got careless outside. At daybreak, Penn woke and contacted the home office to let Clay know what time this fabulous trip on the tundra was supposed to commence so they could keep an eye on the party. A tall lanky guy got issued the rifle. This made Penn wary, but he kept his anxieties concealed. Everyone readied themselves for the trip that would take about 3–4 hours total time. Once underway, they traveled about an hour away from the enclave, a long way from home base. Penn pretended to be jacked out of his mind about the amazing landscape and the beauty and majesty of it all. But all he wanted was to keep an eye on the guy with the gun, get back to base, drink some hot cocoa and take a hot shower. The days were ticking away and Penn just wanted to finish up his interviews, hit his target, write his story and fly the fuck home.

The minute they got within sight of the facility, visibility started to deteriorate. Throughout their excursion, they were equipped with radios and the weather station kept the team leader abreast of the coming fronts. With no geographical barriers and such a large land mass, fronts would come fast and furious and you could be in an awful situation within minutes. As a result–ventures outside the compound to monitor or repair various instruments, as well as flights in and out had to be flexible and well coordinated. You had to remain in constant contact with the base and not go too far or you could get lost and perish. It would be akin to being adrift in space, cut loose from the space station adrift until you died. Standing away from the compound, the blue and white sky with the yellow–white base was amazing to stare at from far away. As they got closer to home you could almost feel the heat and energy humming under the ice and snow. You could feel the fact that there was life out here buried somewhere under the snow. It was definitely the energy that attracted the animals because out here there was absolutely nothing as far as the eye could see, it gave a whole new meaning to the word "desolate."

Penn had never spent so much time on a snow vehicle with big belted tires as he just had. Never in his life did he have occasion before to test the true performance of such specific land gear. But he did have more than a passing familiarity with high powered rifles used for stopping humans and free range predators and in this case, they factored in polar bear stopping potential, note to self. Despite his many exploits in unforgiving environments the world over these situations hit unique watermarks, even for him. The team got back from the day trip where no visitors or polar bears were harmed in the making of the trip.

Experience. There was just no substitute for it. Aria was pacing the floor at home waiting to confirm that no one had been shooting at him and that he had arrived safely back at base and he could chug hot cocoa and get warm again. She was waiting for the big satellite in the sky to tell her everything was going to be okay. Penn, relieved over the successful outing in which he was being watched made his way to his bunk and checked in with Clay. He changed into his workout clothes to hit the gym but first he inhaled some protein bars and a protein shake. At the gym he encountered some of the most overtly bizarre behavior of his entire trip. The guys tended in this environment to be very brusque and territorial–even physical about inflicting pain. They behaved like nasty low land gorillas at the zoo, chest beaters. Penn made it very clear, without using language, that he would not be tolerating that today or for the remainder of his trip. When he was working out he also attracted a few of the more aggressive females who Aria warned him about. One girl even followed him into the locker room. He told her to back off, he wanted to be left alone and get back to his quarters to plan his next few days and get some sleep. She wasn't pleased.

Things had started to get more unsettled and there was a buzz now that existed about his visit. People were starting to take notice and many of them apparently were not happy. It amused him how strident and what bad actors people were. People were either very happy to meet someone from outside or they were upset, territorial and had issues.

Penn had a specific task, to find some folks who had been charged with some very dirty work. These people were passing information to foreign governments and messing with national security at a high level. Whoever these people were, they fit Penn's definitions of scumbag. "All these low level head cases in this frigid ant farm just ticked me off and made me intolerant."

And now that people had started to become overt in their aggressiveness and tried to lord themselves over him; it just pissed him off that much more. Penn took his personal freedom, his personal space internal and external and the use and control of his physical body very seriously; he had worked too hard to attain all of it. And it was what our entire country was built upon. When anyone tried to impede his personal progress by exacting control over him; it became unacceptable very quickly. Penn was not the kind of guy that you wanted to be on the bad side of; you would lose, that's why he was there in the first place, because he did not lose. It was this faith that kept Aria so deeply tied to Penn when he was in the field because she was not in the habit of losing either. She did whatever was necessary was in order to make it work, always. Discomfort in either one of their worlds was never an issue. Both viewed their lives through the prism of taking awful medicine as a child. You just did it. The issue was the outcome, not the discomfort on the way to the outcome.

Penn was sorting, gearing up and weeding out the people who he did not need to be in front of in each department. He packed small quiet weapons, no guns, because even if silenced, they still make noise and there is a scent. Penn needed stealth weapons. His hands and body were quite effective, as were a few other tools of the trade in the advanced edition of spy book 101. He was adept at using all of these tools and did so quite regularly. Penn was quite sure things would get ugly and sooner than he originally thought, Aria had already warned him. That was the constant struggle in the field–you had to be able to assess in real time the unfolding of an assignment as you went along, while you were eyeball deep in it. This was easier to say than to actually execute successfully. Timing is everything; it kept you alive and in one piece during every single mission.

The issue of being too close, of getting too involved, or being emotionally attached was always a danger. It clouded your decision making process and it was almost never a good thing. Penn turned on the television to insure some background noise to obscure any sound that may have come from his quarters because it was time to call Langley and discuss a new plan of attack. The peace of mind that was the rule of the day earlier in the operation was a big benefit now. It made sleep and safety possible and neither could be assured over the next two or three days. Clay and Penn had a decent conversation for the first time in days, thanks to clearer than usual weather.

Penn was convinced that during the interviews over the past few days that he had been "made," and it was now a moral imperative that things move forward. The team was standing by and they were within a 12 hour window. Penn was preparing for closing in on a person that he thought was the target. Not until everything was actually in play would the target become aware. By then it would be too late for the target to do anything about his imminent expiration.

Clay was happy about the progress and was watching the weather because there was a violent storm moving in. Penn and Clay and the team at Langley had been monitoring NOAA, and Clay could now no longer guarantee how everything would stack up including when he would be able to get a team in to extract Penn, when things got very dangerous. Penn would be on his own; he would not have any means of escape for at least 48 hours, maybe longer. There would be nothing anyone could do, period. Once again, it would be another amazing story if Penn managed to get out alive. Aria got the mental brief about the weather. She woke and ran to her computer, checking for updates and to see whether on not she was correct. She went to NOAA and then a handful of satellite photos, she checked sites around the globe. Some of the pictures and video were not even stale yet. All hunches confirmed, Aria saw that he would be stuck.

She knew it would be every operative for himself. Here we go again, she secretly thought to herself. He wouldn't be getting out anytime soon. Aria knew that Clay had just broken the latest news to Penn. Penn and Clay changed the mo of the operation and made a pact; because the clean up team and the transportation specialists were going to be unavailable for comment.

Penn was given the blanket mission statement for, "whatever it takes." From that minute on it became game on and Penn was beyond activated. His forum, duty and it's parameters and any means for accomplishing the goal all shifted and the group blessed him for it. When they wrapped up the conversation, Penn knew what had to be done. He packed his pockets, grabbed his briefcase and went into the hallway. He arrived in the first lab where he was greeted by one of the chicks who had hit on him earlier in week. She walked by him on the way out the door and subtlety gave him the finger to make her point. He smiled once she walked by, because he thought it was funny and oh so typical. He went to see the section director and rapped quietly on his door. He asked to see two different men who worked under him. Penn asked for an empty conference room and had the director contact the first worker. Penn left the outer lab and went up the hallway to an empty conference room. The director sent the first man in to see

169

Penn. The man came in and sat down begrudgingly and got more uncomfortable as Penn asked him a series of probing questions. He was an unimposing Eastern European man who looked like a weasel to Penn. A smallish, pale, fair haired and bespeckled weasel.

When the interview was over the little man scurried out of the room like a rat. Penn heard him through the bug he had planted on him when he walked into the room. The human weasel called his contact the minute he left the meeting. Penn now had confirmation that the second guy who he called for had absolutely no intention of showing up for his "interview". Penn left the room and decided to let the bastards stew. He wanted to see what they would do next. Penn headed for the cafeteria to get some lunch, after which he would do a quick workout to kill the stress. He walked by the window and shook his head, as he could see everything he and Clay discussed. It was crazy white out conditions as far as the eye could see. Penn ate quietly alone in a corner and stuffed some granola and snacks into his pockets to take back to his room. Penn planned his chase as he ate his soup and sandwich, salad and fruit. Just because there were hidden weapons and a license to kill, didn't mean you had to go hungry.

Penn was smart enough to know that after he spoke to this second guy that eating and drinking would become markedly less safe as the hours and days wore on. With no extraction team in place, he knew he had to start bulk loading food. In these type of situations, you had better know who could be aligned with who or who could have access to what departments. Penn knew just how much these people hated him and what a poisoning spree they had been on for a few years around the world. So far he had managed to avoid everything despite being in some very compromising positions.

He went back to his quarters and blew off the idea of the workout. He needed to make things appear normal to everyone else at the compound, so he quickly put in another call to Clay and told him what he intended to do. He dropped off his briefcase and was unpacking when Clay told him the weather would be terrible for the next 12-16 hours. He also told him that the aircraft, one of two planes that had the ability to get in, was having mechanical trouble and it was the only aircraft and proper crew close to his hemisphere. They were getting their hands on the parts and fixing it, but it would be at least 24 hours. He told Penn to "watch his ass and to make sure he got it done." Clay told Penn that he would be monitoring the weather and the entire situation and would advise him of any changes and that he would get him out of there as fast as humanly possible. Clay told Penn he would meet him at the first refueling stop. Penn set up his quarters with a series of devices to make sure his quarters could not be breached without his knowledge. Clay and Penn hung up and agreed on a time to speak again within a few hours. After a quick nap and an electronic alarm tied to Langley, Penn gathered his energies and bolted out of bed and readied himself for his first chess move. To put the weasel and his countryman into play.

Penn emerged into the hallway and started to hunt for his other target, the big fish. After checking a few places Penn found him hiding in one of the more remote bathrooms. He quietly locked the bathroom door so there would be no escape. He confronted the small blondish man. "Is it me or do all these guys look like brothers?" Penn asked him about his position in the whole operation, but the little man would reveal nothing, including his accomplice. It really didn't matter; Penn had already put it together anyway. Still, he did not pull any punches, literally or figuratively. The guy felt so threatened that he tried to get physical. There was almost a scuffle. Penn quietly put a stop to that; with two sharp blows to the head and knocked him out. Penn put his body in a compromising position and propped him up on a commode in a stall and planted an undetectable bug on his person. There was nowhere to run and he had him trapped so Penn had an unusual luxury and would take care of business tomorrow.

Penn would need to find a way out as soon as possible after he sanctioned his target, so it didn't make a whole lot of sense to overreact now. Once he completed his mission there would be no way to deny it and nowhere to go. And who knows, the guy might still fess up and if that happened it would be part of a very different outcome. For now there was no way to tell. These circumstances allowed Penn some breathing room. Penn arranged himself and unlocked the door, left the bathroom and walked down the hall to the chow hall.

He picked up more food and made sure that the cameras caught him as he said hello to some of the nicer people he had met. This established even more time stamps. Penn had been cataloging all the cameras and their movements for 11 days. He knew the location of every camera in the facility at this point. He always engaged in these seemingly benign exercises because he knew the knowledge would come in handy later. He returned to his quarters and shot a text off to tell Clay what was up, and check on the latest flight schedule. Penn spent the evening in his quarters monitoring the bugs he had planted. He also monitored the updates on the weather. Morning came, and Penn awoke with his head on his laptop on the desk in his quarters where he fell asleep listening from the night before. He slept later than he usually ever did and ate in his quarters while he tried to get through to Langley for the late morning travel update. Things would heat up quickly now. Based on all that he heard via the surveillance, he decided that the target was not going to be coming to Jesus anytime soon. So Penn was going to have to stop the bleeding and send him to Jesus, tonight, before he could get anymore intel to the bad guys. He would also have to let Langley know what was going on. This would be the other topic of this days phone calls, that there would be no question about timing which affected Penn's cover being blown and people being left alive to talk about it. To Langley and to Penn that was an unacceptable situation. It would be a moral imperative that he cover all his tracks tonight.

Penn crawled into bed for a few hours for some much deserved horizontal sleep. First he set up the room in case anyone tried to gain entry while he was asleep and vulnerable. Then he shot Aria a text and drifted off. Aria was up pacing ahead of the storm, concentrating on helping Penn and finally getting past the hubbub of Christmas. Aria knew what was coming and she spent time putting out the energy while Clay and his team did the prep work for Penn being under it again in a few hours. Clay was hurriedly getting the airplanes online and coordinated for the swoop and scoop and the rendezvous at the first refueling stop. Aria wanted everything to go perfectly, it had to. There was a very small safety window because of the nature of the whole operation. Aria had no input from Penn and was trying desperately to set up his homecoming. In her mind's eye, she could see how he was getting out. She was just a little fuzzy on exactly when, but that would become clearer over the next few hours as she concentrated more on Penn and on Clay's behavior.

CHAPTER TWENTY-FOUR

A few hours passed and Penn shook himself awake. Aria took a deep breath and almost fell over. She knew he was awake and they were online. It was game on. This was the first moment when everything came together. Within hours everything would culminate. Aria had been working from home today so she was able to drop what she had been working on and change rooms; she didn't want the distraction of the office or phones or the news feed and computers buzzing in the back round. Penn sat up in bed and all but jumped up to pee and shower at the exact same moment. He stepped into the shower quickly finished, toweled off and ate a protein bar. He knocked back some oj while he planned the backup to his backup weapon. He packed a small black bag and put his all weather gear into the bag to hide it. After stuffing food into his inside pockets, he shot Clay a text. Then he sent Aria a text, and told her "I love you" It had a half hour delay getting to her but she already knew where he was headed. Penn left the room in many grey, white and black layers ready for anything. He found the candidate in a far flung lab on the outskirts of the compound, cowering like an animal.

It was the middle of the facilities night and the crews that were on duty were lean. Penn planned it that way. He pulled a full Sahlahi, crashing the party and it made select people in the compound uneasy. Penn took pleasure in knocking the bad guys out of their comfort zone. He entered the lab and of course John was the only guy there, hiding out amongst the test tubes. A scuffle ensued but Penn was careful not to make any noise or break glass. Sound travels in the dead of night in concrete and metal boxes underground in the middle of nowhere. He could not afford a screw-up, not today. Penn put the bad guy down silently. He would no longer be selling secrets that didn't belong to him. Penn felt good about it. This facility existed to keep the world safe, not to assist in making it less so. By now, Tim and the rescue fly boys were about an hour out and the weather was breaking and bumpy. They were flying in between fronts, just as Clay had planned. It was grey blue, white hazy other worldly outside and as dark as it got.

Aria was pacing and breathing hard. She knew what was going down. Penn threw his unconscious adversary over his shoulder and took him to a snowmobile that he had hidden around the back of the compound. He strapped him to the vehicle and double checked the full gas tank. Then he cranked it up and pointed the nose towards the base of the mountains in the distance. And on the exhale the breath froze coming out of his mouth. He looked around and carefully pulled away, he timed his departure to avoid the prying eyes of the compounds remote cameras.

As he sped away from the compound and into the middle of no where, he was never so aware of his own mortality in his whole life. But he felt a surge of warmth and electrical energy rush through his core, he knew by now that the source was Aria. She always helped, she was right there. She never let him do anything alone, and he no longer wanted to. They had yet another moment of being strangely and uniquely connected across the miles in an utterly primal, focused, frightening and private survival moment.

Penn had to make this snowmobile run and he had to be successful. The plans had changed and it was up to him to clean up the mess for the world. It was insanely scary out there and Penn felt small and insignificant. He went 25 minutes to the base of the mountain range before the snow was too deep to ride further, and when it got that way he pointed the snowmobile north and went a few miles more. Then he slowed and came to stop and made sure John met someone's maker. Penn dumped the body in the snow and was sure to put enough snow around the little man to camouflage the shape. Penn thought always that john could have made a choice to go another way; but sadly most of his targets chose the path of greatest resistance. Penn thought it was a selfish choice many times. And he was pretty sure that after Jesus found out what the bad guy tried to pull off that he wouldn't be the guy waiting for John when he arrived in the afterlife. Penn put a couple of shots in the corpse to hurry the process along and ring the dinner bell for the polar bears and wolves.

He knew that he had to high tail it back to the compound and it wouldn't be very long before a family of polar bears got up close and personal with what was left of John. Ahhh, the circle of life he thought, if it had to be like this at least it helped some life form. He thought about how he came to his job description. He didn't automatically get in, it's a position that you just sort of arrive at. You would have to be immensely fucked up to have a proclivity for it, and that wasn't him; not even when they really deserved it. To save lives and help the world not to go to hell if there is one, he thought. Penn looked around at the majesty of the frigid natural surroundings and the otherworldly dark grey sky. He would never forget how it cast an eerie pallor on the winter white landscape. After one last look around, Penn straddled the snow mobile and blasted off once again, lit only by the moon and the glow on the horizon he retraced his route. The wind started to pick up to a howl as if everything bigger than him was mocking the smallness of humanity. The speed and the sting of the air bit through his face-mask and gel covering. With the adrenaline starting to slow as he got closer to survival and base camp, he could feel everything that he did not have the luxury of noticing on the trip out. Within a few hours the sun would rise higher in the sky and it would look like any day in sparkling downtown Anchorage, glistening and white light clear, just minus the cars and the fast food joints and the lumber jack looking men in plaid, black, red or tan camo. It started to snow ever so gently and Penn became keenly aware of the frigid air in his lungs as the engine of the little machine that he rode like a horse and how it screamed in the thin air and barren ice and snow.

Back at home, Aria was sitting on her bed slowly coming down, breathing slowly filling her little lungs in one slow steady shallow

pull; fully aware of what Penn was feeling and seeing the body laying abandoned in the snow, a necessary cast off waiting for nature
to reclaim it in one way or another. The bad guy was now a "polar
bear drive through" as Aria put it to Penn. That was the only thing
that closed out Aria's thought of the whole series of events. Aria
was wide eyed with the details of the whole operation. She was
counting down the minutes until Penn got back inside at the compound. Safe and warm. Back in Virginia, Clay was busy getting into
an unmarked government airplane. The fly boys had just contacted
the tower or what was used as the tower at base camp and notified them that they would be on the ground in about 25 minutes.
Tim was communicating with the tower requesting back-up and a
crew to help unload and reload the bird so he could complete his
objective in due course picking up his special delivery, Penn. They
would be refueling the minute they hit the pack ice. The recovery
team would literally land, gather supplies and mail, use the toilet,
eat on the fly stuffing their pockets with non perishables, pour in
some coffee or cocoa and collect their precious cargo, Penn. The
snow was coming down lightly when they pulled in and visibility
was good, for now. Captain Tim was not naive enough to think
that things would stay this hospitable on any level.

Penn had been back for about 10 minutes and he had stashed
the snowmobile and made a beeline for his quarters. He had to
communicate quickly with Clay and let Langley know that they
were in good stead. He showered to warm his body back to reality.
He quickly packed and went to the mess hall to make sure that he
had been seen by the scientists and all the video surveillance. He
swallowed some turkey sausage and some eggs. He missed Aria
and he still couldn't warm up, so he was drinking as much tea
and cocoa as his body could hold. He was dunking his toast when
captain Tim and the team walked into the mess hall. He was never
so happy to see people he cared about. He looked up to ask Tim
when they were leaving, but he still had to play it cool.

Penn let them know that he was ready when they were. He did
not want there to be any miscommunication. Tim had Penn's back

and he knew that often times there were "hot ops" and he was a semi unwitting partner. He was there to get Penn out proto, end of story. Captain Tim did not know what the operation involved, it was need to know only. He just knew he was supposed to deliver Penn to the rendezvous point where Clay would be waiting. Penn excused himself and went to bid the facility director farewell. He also had to call Clay and let him know they were leaving. In under an hour they were all on the flight line, and Penn was silently jumping up and down with glee. Penn was hot as hell as it would only be a short time before people started looking for the agent who was now serving as polar bear bait. Penn was over this ice palace and wanted out asap

Everyone in the crew boarded the ski equipped C130. The pilots did their last minute flight checks. Penn strapped himself in and said a silent prayer. He hated flying as a rule and especially under these lousy conditions, but still he was grateful to be leaving safely and with a full belly. He was curious to see how long that happiness about his breakfast lasted. Things had been going so well today that he wasn't feeling particularly confident. Under these flying conditions it could go either way. The men buckled in to their 3 point harness style seatbelts and you could see the relief on everyone's face at the click of each individual seat belt and as the engine screamed and roared in the thin cold air. Tim pointed the nose in the direction of civilization and the sigh in the cabin was almost audible. The crew and the passengers were cleared by the tower for takeoff and the Captain guided the aircraft down the icy makeshift runway. The engines revved hard one last time as Captain Tim forced the plane into the sky and as it climbed he retracted the gear. After a short period of time the turbulence became apparent. Then "apparent" turned into a very nasty front that there was no way to go around, under or over. So Captain Tim with no place to go decided that going through was their best shot. Shortly after Tim and the team committed themselves to their fate, everyone on the plane got violently airsick. The turbulence was terrible. It was the single worst flight even these seasoned veterans had ever encountered. Even Tim started having thoughts about another crash landing. There were some morbid moments. There was a great deal of silence mixed with some very creative swear words.

Everyone lost the entire contents of their stomachs one by one. The inside of the plane became a mixture that smelled like extreme biology and primal fear. Dry heaves moved each man's body unapologetically like a massive invisible god like puppeteer. The flight had been frightening and violent. When they finally landed to refuel, they all would have liked to have spent the night. But they had a schedule of fly overs that they had to keep. It was all very carefully timed. Penn wanted to text Aria and tell her about everything that was happening and that they were okay, surprisingly; but Clay who was also in the air advised him against it. Aria would have to wait until the next refueling stop where he would meet Clay before she had cyberspace confirmation of everyone's safety. At the refueling stop Penn said his goodbyes to Captain Tim and the recovery team and they had a good laugh about everyone losing their lunch and their breakfast and god only knows what else. But unlike last time, Captain Tim was able to keep the airplane in the air. Just when you think someone cannot get any more talented... Penn didn't have to rescue his rescuers and then as if on que, Clay and his team met Penn to lead him out to yet another flight line where a small private jet was patiently waiting for them. They boarded the beautiful jet for a short hop to a safe place where they would spend the night and de- brief before they returned to Washington the next day. They spent one night on the way home doing research for the next field trip.

Clay and Penn had learned from each other very quickly that they both were mindful of the fact that they were on the federal payroll. It would have been better to stay an extra night and catch their breath, but contrary to popular belief, these case officers were monumentally respectful of who was paying the bills. In fact, they were much more aware of that than most federal workers, because they understood what it was like to be stuck in a foreign land with no resources. This was not a concept that most Americans would ever become familiar with.

Aria slept that night like a baby, but she was so excited she could have popped. Last night as she was getting into bed, she had received a call from Clay as he was boarding his first flight. She was half asleep when she spoke to him and so she fell back into a deep sleep. Despite the interruption she woke ridiculously early and remembered the middle of the night conversation the night before with Clay. For a moment she wondered if it had really taken place. So she woke and packed and prepped to board a flight later in the day bound for Reagan National Airport in Washington. She looked at the note she wrote for herself in the dark to jolt her memory about the details. She wrote down the time and the airline, that was it. When she arrived at the airport a ticket was waiting in her name and there was a round shiny faced man behind the counter that seemed to know who she was, as if he had been expecting her.

The direct flight was uneventful and short, just the way Aria liked it and then when she arrived at baggage claim she retrieved her bag and scurried out to the curb to see a large unmarked government vehicle pull up and stop right in front of her. A door flew open the minute it glided silently to a stop and a nameless man that she had never seen before greeted her by name and confirmed why he was there. Aria threw her bag in the back ahead of her and she and the silent man made the 45-mintue drive to Andrews Air Force Base. By now it was getting late and the sun was on the far side of set. It gets dark early at this time of year Aria thought, much earlier than home. The lights to mark the season were reflecting in the snow. It looked like a big white blanket had been pulled over the greater Washington metropolitan area and the sky was so clear that Aria thought that it looked like the stars were a place where someone poked holes in a light bright.

Their departure from near the city at night looked like Christmas special footage, snow falling and covering everything like a capital winter postcard. She thought about how it must have looked in Washington when the monuments were new. Breathtaking. She knew Penn was glued to his window for the flight as they flew in over the DC area. They had missed the Holiday together, so Penn was melancholy. Penn had no idea what Clay had arranged and he thought he was coming home after Christmas to an empty house. Clay knew what he had to do; he had arranged to have Aria deposited with a handler onto their airstrip.

The nameless man and Aria were waived onto base and after a short security check they rolled right out on to the service road adjacent to the active runway. Their black vehicle surrounded by crisp white snow; it covered anything that was out in the elements, people, planes, cars, hangers. The car stopped and the driver opened the door for Aria. She was still amazed with where Clay managed to position her. Before she even had time to understand the full impact of where she was or what was really happening, Clay and Penn pulled up in a small long range executive jet. The jet rolled to a stop as the ground crew scurried in the light snow. Illuminated by the lights from the vehicle, steps dropped from the door of the aircraft. Out came Penn in a black down company issued jacket looking tired, rumpled and feeling hungry. He was followed closely by Clay who was dressed in the same basic gear with a large black pack over his shoulder. Aria could barely believe her eyes. Penn's face lit up as he figured out that this was not exhaustion, hunger or jet lag playing games with his heart. As he descended onto the tarmac Aria was there to greet him… Merry Christmas he thought to himself and he looked back at Clay. Aria slowly approached him and buried her tear stained face in his chest. He wrapped his entire body around her as snow flakes fell all around and once again Aria found herself enveloped in the arms of a man in a little southern town called Washington. "Merry Christmas Buddy" was all that Clay said.

ACKNOWLEGDEMENTS

There are a few people that I would like to acknowledge that I could not have done this without. Friends and family, associates, mentors and colleagues, some gone but never forgotten, beloved all. Thank you for everything.

M&D, A, A, AG, SG, H, MT, G&P, J, PJ, JP the chess master of TO,RG,SS,K&K&P,SS,Colonel,LRP,Tra,Scissors,AMc,UE&AM,I& KM&A,BT,WM,SV,JT,RG,HG,JM,AA,GN,AT,DO,GDP,GK,V,D,M, WB,FL,JP,LD,PMGS,SG&MB,GW,Ran,Bre,S,D,H,TNG,RR,C,G,K &K,Wolp,MH,TD,SW,C, N & C S,Bre,MG,S,C,Min,JM,MR,LG,Che, PB,Mc,DC,BB,Cr,Kat, Cooter and anyone else that in haste I may have over-looked. I beg your forgiveness. You know who you are.

Look for the next book in the series by Birgit Von Schondorf
Coming soon!

The Alphabet Games "SOL" Speed of Light
(T.A.G. book 2)
RPFP

Follow updates for The Alphabet Games

@thealphabetgames
Like us on FB
Thealphabetgames.com

www.ingramcontent.com/pod-product-compliance
Lightning Source LLC
Chambersburg PA
CBHW070006300526
45794CB00001B/214